TAMING YOUR GREMLIN

Also by Richard D. Carson

NEVER GET A TATTOO

TAMING YOUR GREMLIN

a guide to
Enjoying Yourself

by
Richard D. Carson

illustrations by
Novle Rogers

 HarperPerennial
A Division of HarperCollins*Publishers*

Dedication

*to my wife, Leti, and our son, Jonah — my sidekicks
who have tapped into
what seems to be a boundless love within me;
and
to Maharaji, who showed me the source of that love.*

A hardcover edition of this work was published by The Family Resource, Inc. It is here reprinted by arrangement with the author.

TAMING YOUR GREMLIN. Copyright © 1983 by Richard David Carson. All rights reserved. Printed in the United States of America. No part of this book may be used or reproduced in any manner whatsoever without written permission except in the case of brief quotations embodied in critical articles and reviews. For information address Harper & Row, Publishers, Inc., 10 East 53rd Street, New York, N.Y. 10022

First PERENNIAL LIBRARY edition published 1986. Reissued 1990.

Library of Congress Cataloging-in-Publication Data
Carson, Richard David
  Taming your gremlin.

  Reprint. Originally published: Dallas, Tex. : Family Resource, 1983.
  1. Happiness. 2. Success. 3. Self-perception. 4. Choice (Psychology) I. Title
BF575.H27C38 1986   158'.1   86-45310
ISBN 0-06-096102-3 (pbk.)

05 04 03 02   RRD(H) 40 39 38 37 36 35 34

Acknowledgments

I want to thank my friend Roland Arthur. This book might not have come about in this form at this time were it not for his confidence in me, and I am most appreciative.

And I want to thank Paige Thompson. When she first opened a copy of this book she also opened herself to it. In consulting on the layout and design of the original version, she performed not only as a fine technician but as the gifted artist she is.

I am especially grateful to my mother, Eva, my dad, Al, in whose memory this book is written, and to my brother, Frank. The three of them had a good thing going prior to my birth, and when I came along they welcomed me into the environment of love and acceptance they were already enjoying. I recall comedy and clashes, joyful howls and occasional scowls, semi-lean times and ultra-keen times—but it was that infallible, pervasive love that made it so nice. I felt both safe and free there with them, and this fact of my existence seems somehow basic to my having the following perspective to offer.

Contents

Chapter 3

Chapter 4

CHOOSING AND PLAYING WITH OPTIONS 68

Chapter 5

BEING IN PROCESS

Chapter 6

FOR KICKS

Chapter 7

THE PLEASANT PERSON ACT

Chapter 8

A FINAL WORD

TAMING YOUR GREMLIN

INTRODUCING

THE BOOK, ME, YOU, and YOUR GREMLIN

THE BOOK

This book is not intended to guide you to enlightenment, to eternal bliss, or to riches. It will, however, help you to enjoy yourself more and more each day. It is simple and practical and I hope that reading it brings you much pleasure.

ME

Over the last 20 or so years a number of people have come to me for counseling. They have come with a variety of "presenting problems" including anxiety (experienced all sorts of ways), strange behavior, and strained relationships. While my service to them could be described in clinical, philosophical, and perhaps even metaphysical terms, the truth is that I have spent most of my time with them simply helping them improve their ability to enjoy themselves. I have had the pleasure of seeing not only individuals, but couples and entire families enhance their potential for day-to-day, moment-to-moment enjoyment, and in the process, for most of them anyway, their "presenting problems" have disappeared. Those who themselves were "helping professionals" such as physicians, teachers, ministers, and psychologists tell me that increasing their ability to enjoy themselves has contributed to an increase in their effectiveness with those whom they serve.

I am no master of the art of self-enjoyment. I am, however, a conscientious student of the process and I am steadily becoming more and more proficient not only at enjoying myself, but at assisting others to do the same.

YOU

Having commented on what this book is and is not, and on who I am and am not, let me say a word about who you are and are not. You probably already know, or at least sense, that you are not your body, your feelings, your thoughts, your personality, or even some complex combination of these variables. Furthermore, you are not the roles you play such as mother, father, wife, friend, up-person, down-person, client, counselor, all-around good person, or low-down nogoodnik. These are just labels to describe your style of existence at any point in time. The real you is a pure life force and is not limited by your concepts and ideas about who you are. It is the real you that is able to experience and enjoy the body in which you dwell, the external physical world in which you live, and the thoughts, memories and fantasies your brain creates and stores. I do not know all that there is to know about the real you (or the real me, for that matter), but I have experienced enough to know that the real you is beautiful beyond your most creative fantasy, and allowed to do so it will guide the evolvement of your life in a manner that will feel terrific.

The real you feels wonderful all of the time; therefore, the more you are able to allow the real you complete freedom, the more you will enjoy yourself. This may sound simple. That is because it is. But it is not easy. For while you were created capable of complete and constant enjoyment, there is within you a gremlin intent on squelching your very essence and consequently your level of enjoyment.

YOUR GREMLIN

You already have some sense of your gremlin though you may have never focused your awareness on him or labeled him. Your gremlin is the narrator in your head. He has influenced you since you came into this world and he accompanies you throughout this entire existence. He is with you when you wake up in the morning and when you go to sleep at night. He tells you who and how you are, and he defines and interprets your every experience. He wants you to

3

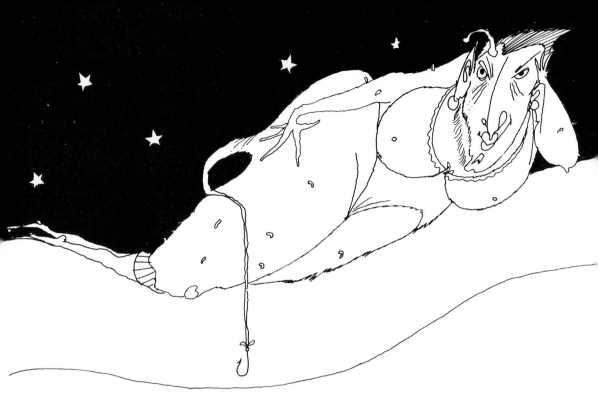

accept his interpretations as reality, and his goal from moment-to-moment, day-to-day, is to squelch the real, vibrant you within. I am not sure of the factors that contributed to the make-up of your particular gremlin. I am sure, however, that he was created, at least in part, by your past experiences.

Your gremlin wants you to feel bad and he carries out this loathsome pursuit via sophisticated maneuvers, which we will discuss later, and by convincing you to waste time reliving the past, worrying about the future, and analyzing the relationships between all sorts of people and things. He wants you to believe that he has your best interest at heart and that his primary purpose is to serve and protect you. His motive is actually much less honorable. He is intent on making you feel lousy. His caution about life and living is inordinate and his methods of control are over-zealous. If by chance you are familiar with theories of

4

psychotherapy take note that your gremlin is not the parent ego-state of Eric Berne's transactional analysis, the Top Dog of Fritz Perl's gestalt therapy, or the super-ego of Sigmund Freud's psychoanalytic theory. He is not merely a part of your psychological make-up. He is a GREMLIN and his personality, like his dastardly intention, is all his own. One thing is for certain, as you begin to *simply notice* your gremlin, you will become acutely sensitive to the fact that you are not your gremlin, but rather his observer. You will see clearly that your gremlin has no real hold on you. As this awareness develops, you will begin to enjoy yourself more and more. It is to you, the observer, that this book is written.

SIMPLY NOTICING

The "simply" in "simply noticing" cannot be overstated. Simply noticing has nothing to do with analyzing, understanding, predicting the future, or undoing the past. Simply noticing involves only *simply noticing.*

TRYING AND FIGURING OUT

I hope that you will not try to figure out the gist of what I am saying, for both "trying" and "figuring out" are a waste of time. To try and/or figure out is to invite your gremlin into our relationship. Two is company and three is a crowd especially if the third party is a gremlin. Besides, what I have to say to you is none of his business. Instead of trying and/or figuring out, simply relax and breathe comfortably, noticing what you are reading. If you get bored, confused, overwhelmed, distracted, or spaced out, simply stop for a while.

2

MORE ABOUT GREMLINS

Gremlins are very sophisticated and have developed elaborate styles of blocking the natural excited vibrant soul within each of us. As you increase your awareness of your own gremlin, you may actually develop some appreciation for his creativity. My choice to use a male pronoun in general reference to gremlins grows out of my very intimate (not to be confused with enjoyable) relationship with my own gremlin, who most often presents himself as a male. I say "most often" because gremlins change not only their sex, but their entire personality from moment to moment and from situation to situation. Your gremlin can appear as your best friend and advisor or as your grossest most ill-intentioned enemy. Regardless of his appearance he must be observed. Left to do his own will he will make you miserable. He may allow you occasional highs, but most often he will lead you into periods of intense anxiety, sadness, anger, and eventually, emptiness.

GREMLINS I HAVE MET

Many of my clients have come to know their gremlins so well that they have developed their abilities to visualize them. They tell me that this has been an aid in helping them to tame their gremlins. A few of the gremlins my clients have introduced me to are described below. Your gremlin may resemble any or all of these, but I assure you that his style of making you miserable will be unique. After all, he has known you for years and has developed sophisticated maneuvers for squelching the natural lovable you within.

Gremlins are far more complex than these few examples indicate. Those I have met have had an impressive repertoire of methods for engendering misery. Each, however, seems to have a preferred strategy.

"The General"

Jack is 32. He is a financially successful attorney whose battles with his gremlin have left him with an ulcer. His gremlin is short, stout, bald, straight-backed, and wears a military uniform. He insists that Jack lead life in accordance with a complex scheme of rules, regulations, shoulds, and ought-to's. He has Jack clearly convinced that were it not for his (the gremlin's) advice, Jack would be a slug-like, ineffectual mamma's boy. When I met Jack he had big biceps, a black belt in Karate, and an inability to get an erection.

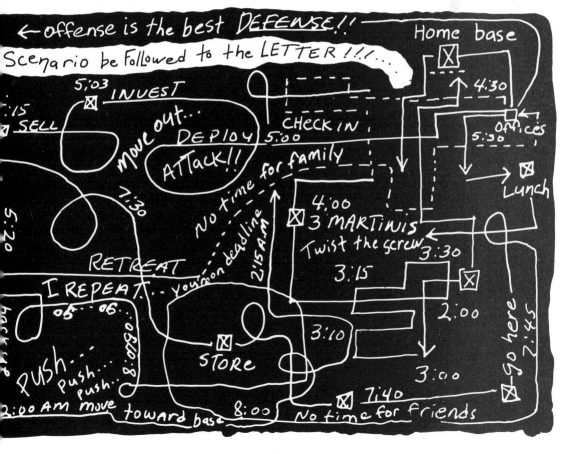

BON APPetit Monsieur...

"The Artist"

Joseph is a 40-year-old psychologist whose gremlin tries to convince him that unless his (the gremlin's) advice is followed, Joseph will finally become destitute and lonely. From time to time Joseph's gremlin shows him a beautiful painting entitled: "Joseph Leading a Happy Life." He convinces Joseph that fulfillment, happiness, and general comfort with himself will result once he has arranged his circumstances and the people in his life into a living version of the beautiful painting. Joseph has noticed that over time his gremlin has altered the composition of the beautiful painting. He has further noticed that this usually happens about the time he gets close to matching his life to the painting. This leaves Joseph feeling somewhat like the proverbial horse who follows the carrot. When Joseph sought me out he was taking his third post-doctoral psychology residency and was considering suicide.

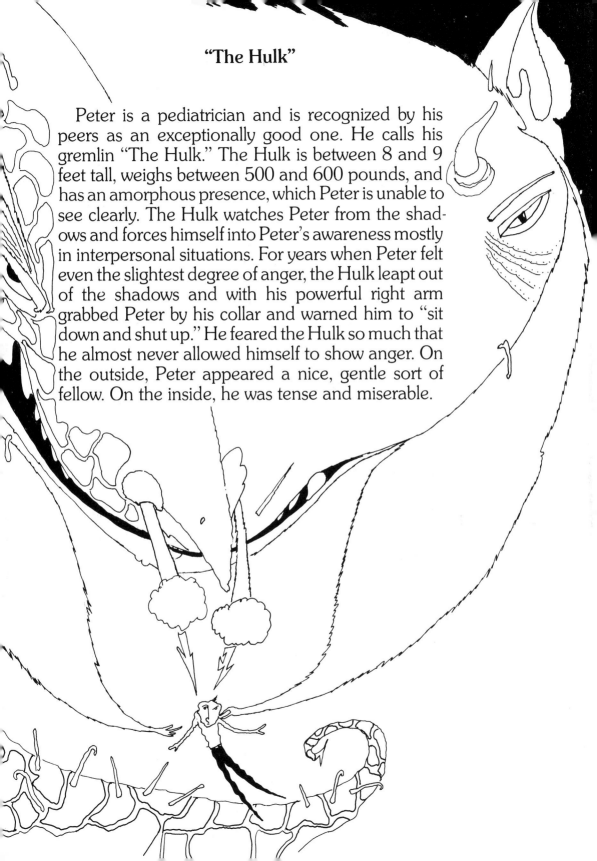

"The Hulk"

Peter is a pediatrician and is recognized by his peers as an exceptionally good one. He calls his gremlin "The Hulk." The Hulk is between 8 and 9 feet tall, weighs between 500 and 600 pounds, and has an amorphous presence, which Peter is unable to see clearly. The Hulk watches Peter from the shadows and forces himself into Peter's awareness mostly in interpersonal situations. For years when Peter felt even the slightest degree of anger, the Hulk leapt out of the shadows and with his powerful right arm grabbed Peter by his collar and warned him to "sit down and shut up." He feared the Hulk so much that he almost never allowed himself to show anger. On the outside, Peter appeared a nice, gentle sort of fellow. On the inside, he was tense and miserable.

"Big Ugly"

The first time I relaxed enough to visualize my gremlin he presented himself as about 10 feet tall and incredibly ugly. He was part dragon and part human with short arms and very strong hind legs which allowed him to stand up. He is less ominous and a bit more mellow now, but he still loves to force me to pay attention to him. He likes to engage me in battle and once I am engaged he picks at me with statements intended to engender self-doubt and worry. To date, my gremlin has not smashed me or eaten me alive or driven me mad, but on occasion he tries to convince me that he has the power to do so. He still tends to make such a hullabaloo when he wants my attention that I find myself wasting some of my life energy grappling with him.

"The Coach"

Dale is a wholesale salesman. He is 27, extremely handsome, a hard worker, and wealthy (because of his hard work). When we initially came in contact he worked so hard and moved so fast that I was surprised that he found the time to put so many things in his mouth. He smoked 3 packages of cigarettes a day, had 2 or 3 martinis at lunch, and drank several cocktails every evening. I asked him not to smoke during our time together, which aroused his gremlin to such an extent that he raised his head in fury. This gave Dale and me an opportunity to "simply notice" him. Subsequently, Dale labeled his gremlin "The Coach." I am glad he chose that name because Dale's gremlin resembled a coach I once had.

Most of the coaches I have had have been either big and burly or little and feisty. The coach that Dale's gremlin reminded me of was of the little and feisty variety. I never saw my feisty coach walk or sit. He was always running or jogging. As he ran he would be shouting things like "Lotta hustle, gang," or "Go, go, go," or "Be number one." Sometimes he would just yell noises like "Hubba, hubba, hubba." He never made much sense but he had a knack for getting people moving. As a matter of fact it was almost impossible to be still when you were around him. Dale's gremlin is very much like this coach. Dale sees him as having a whistle around his neck, as being short, thin, strong, and not so much fast as quick. He uses the same sort of words that my coach used with emphasis on the "Be number one!" For years he had Dale convinced that the world was a race and that Dale needed to win it. Dale was so busy

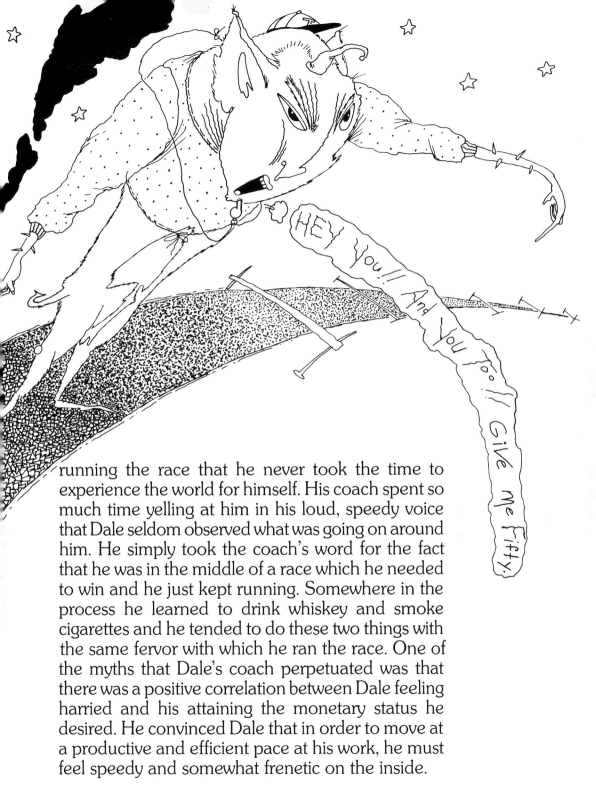

running the race that he never took the time to experience the world for himself. His coach spent so much time yelling at him in his loud, speedy voice that Dale seldom observed what was going on around him. He simply took the coach's word for the fact that he was in the middle of a race which he needed to win and he just kept running. Somewhere in the process he learned to drink whiskey and smoke cigarettes and he tended to do these two things with the same fervor with which he ran the race. One of the myths that Dale's coach perpetuated was that there was a positive correlation between Dale feeling harried and his attaining the monetary status he desired. He convinced Dale that in order to move at a productive and efficient pace at his work, he must feel speedy and somewhat frenetic on the inside.

"The Reverend"

Katherine is 40. Her gremlin looks like her grand-father only he wears a ministerial collar and engages her by preaching to her from the New Testament. He especially likes to make appearances when Katherine is having sex with someone. Until Katherine began to tame her gremlin she was not only good and righteous, but lonely, emotionally isolated, and unable to have an orgasm.

Sex, sex, sex, tsk, tsk, tsk . . . tsk.

"The Grim Reaper"

Dorothy is 34, married, and the mother of three children. Her life-style resembles a modified version of the "Father Knows Best" TV series of the '50's. Her living situation looks to others almost exactly as she wants it to. When Dorothy came to see me she was spending her time taking her children to school, cleaning house, going to the grocery store, watching television, and suffering almost constant, barely tolerable, emotional pain. I have met many people with gremlins similar to Dorothy's. It is strange but true that there are vast numbers of people walking around on the planet who believe that feeling hassled, disgruntled, bummed-out, low-down and simply "in a funk" is a natural way of being. For some people this is the only style of existence they know. This was the case with Dorothy. Having problems and worrying was her way of life. In a sense it was her entertainment. She spent a great deal of time in a world of make-believe analyzing situations, fearing the future, and regretting the past. While she felt far less than terrific, on some level she was comfortable. Worrying kept her occupied and allowed her to avoid making contact with the real world; for it is impossible to be lost in worry about the future and/or the past and fully relate to the real world at the same time.

Some of the emotional sufferers I have met even use suffering as a basis for relationships (not to be confused with friendships). I have known people whose relationships with others revolve entirely around their helping one another with whatever hassles are current for them. Dorothy's Grim Reaper perpetuated the notion that suffering was not only natural, but noble. He sometimes taunted her with the promise

17

that suffering in the present would lead her to contentment at a later date.

For Dorothy to choose to do something other than emotionally suffer was very difficult. Like most people who are enmeshed with a Grim Reaper or the like, she was unaware of her habit of suffering. She was, we might say, "in it." She did not realize her control over how she felt or her ability to choose to enjoy herself and her life. Gremlins who take the form of the Grim Reaper are vicious and tenacious. They can, however, be tamed. Later we will discuss the gremlin taming process.

Your gremlin may portray characteristics common to these few examples. Remember, however, that gremlins have a chameleon-like ability to change their disguises and their methods. Your gremlin has most assuredly developed several styles of being that are especially catered to his attack on you.

18

GREMLIN MYTHS

You may have noticed from these few examples that gremlins tend to perpetuate myths about people, life, and the nature of the universe. Often the myths they use to cloud our pure experience have been around for so long and are so much a part of our existence that we are unaware of them. So that you might become sensitized to some of your own gremlin's myths, I have listed below some of the most common myths perpetuated by gremlins I have met in the last few months:

1. Your true self is unlovable.
2. You can only enjoy yourself for short periods of time.
3. Fast is good and slow is bad.
4. To show sadness is to be weak or child-ish or unreliable or overly dependent.
5. Nice girls don't enjoy sex.
6. Nice girls certainly don't show that they enjoy sex.
7. Asking for what you want is selfish.
8. To show anger is to be sinful, childish, unprofessional, and/or out of control.
9. To express uncensored joy is to be silly or unprofessional.
10. Not acknowledging and/or not express-ing feelings will make them go away.
11. Something terrible is going to happen.
12. Men are better leaders than women.

and the cruelest myths of all:

13. Worry has value.
14. Anxiety has value.
15. Guilt has value.

As you become more and more astute at simply noticing your gremlin you will become aware of the myths he uses to dampen your happiness. Some may be obvious to you already. You may want to jot them down. For this purpose, I have included, at the end of this book, several blank sheets of paper.

A FEW WORDS ABOUT
THE GREMLIN TAMING PROCESS

Taming your gremlin is a simple (not to be confused with easy) process. Taming your gremlin can be an enjoyable process. Taming your gremlin takes practice and persistence. Taming your gremlin requires the sort of effort implied by words like "allowing" and "letting" not by words like "trying" and "straining." There are three basic processes involved in taming your gremlin. These are:

SIMPLY NOTICING

CHOOSING AND
PLAYING WITH OPTIONS

and

BEING IN PROCESS

3

SIMPLY NOTICING

To simply notice is to be aware — to pay attention. Simply noticing has nothing to do with asking yourself why you are like you are although these answers will become obvious to you as you pay attention to yourself. In taming your gremlin it is important to simply notice *how* you are, not *why* you are how you are. "Thinking about" and "simply noticing" are very different processes. "Thinking about" is the preferred activity of your gremlin and the product of your gremlin's uptightness about not being able to completely understand and control you and the universe. "Simply noticing" on the other hand is what happens when you experience yourself and your surroundings *without* inputs from your gremlin. "Thinking about" removes you from your current experience. "Simply noticing" puts you in contact with your current experience. "Simply noticing" is more exciting and productive than "thinking about." When you are simply noticing, you can love and create naturally and fully. When you are thinking about, you are anything but creative. Simply noticing is the first and most important step in the gremlin taming process. Let us call your ability to simply notice your "Awareness."

21

AWARENESS

Awareness is a tool. At any point in time you can choose to focus your awareness on your body, on the world around you via your sensory receptors, or on your thoughts, fantasies, ideas, and/or memories. When you focus your awareness on your body or on what you are directly experiencing with your sensory receptors you are grounded in reality. When, however, you focus your awareness on your thoughts, fantasies, ideas, and memories, you are involved in the "world of make-believe." In the world of make-believe you can spend time reliving the past, rehearsing for the future, predicting the future, attempting to make meaning out of what you notice about your body or the world around you, or simply entertaining yourself. To dwell in the world of make-believe is neither good nor bad. It can, in fact, be productive to learn from the past or to plan for the future. Certainly, fantasy can be very entertaining and it is necessary in order for creativity to occur. To lead a full rich life, however, and to enjoy yourself, it will be helpful to be conscious of the flow of your awareness from your body—to the world as you experience it with your sensory receptors—to the world of make-believe.

Sometimes we unconsciously slip into the world of make-believe. If, for example, you and I were talking right now and I saw you looking at me, I might imagine that you were listening to me, or that you were bored, or that you were angry with me, or any combination of these, or who knows what? I might even predicate my actions on my fantasy. If I imagined that you were listening to me I probably would continue talking. If I imagined that you were bored, I might stop talking. If I imagined that you were angry with me I might get uptight and begin communicating with you very defensively. My action would be based on make-believe fantasy and my fantasy would in all likelihood be based on past experiences rather than on the reality of the current moment.

Taming your gremlin does not involve withdrawing yourself from the world of make-believe. It simply involves making certain that you enter the world of make-believe by *choice* rather than by habit.

Your awareness will serve you best when you gently focus it. Words like "spaced-out" or "foggy" describe your existence when your awareness is not focused. Being "spaced out" is no more than generalizing your awareness, that is, taking in too much at once. A key word when it comes to focusing your awareness is SLOW. Another key word is NOTICING.

Many people grow up believing that their awareness extends only to those boundaries defined by the limits of their sensory receptors. Other people have expanded their awareness beyond their physical senses. Some people have, for example, developed clairvoyant abilities. Whether or not your awareness is expanded beyond your physical senses is totally irrelevant when it comes to taming your gremlin and enjoying yourself. Regardless of how expansive or how limited your senses are, you must still learn to gently focus your awareness if you are to tame your gremlin. The first step in taming your gremlin is to simply notice him at work. Awareness is a tool for doing just that. Your awareness will help you differentiate yourself from your gremlin.

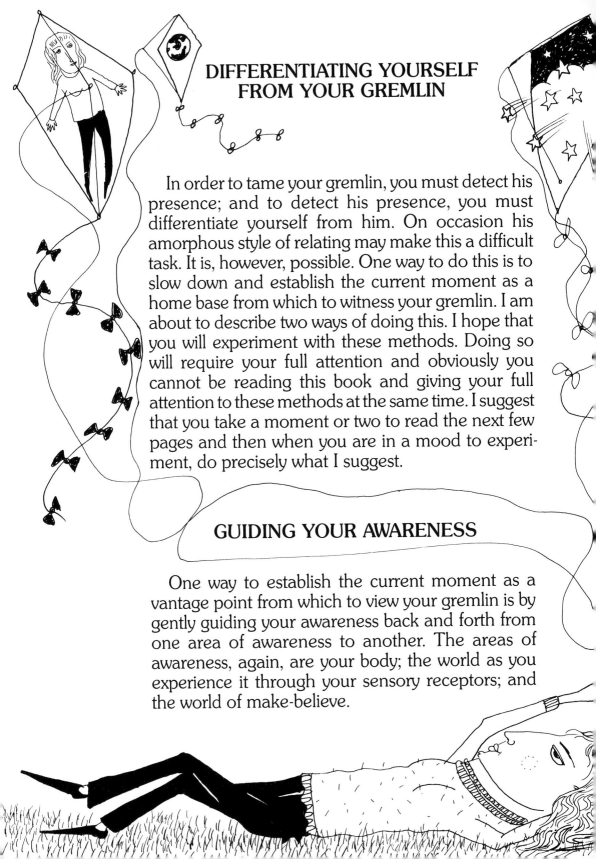

DIFFERENTIATING YOURSELF
FROM YOUR GREMLIN

In order to tame your gremlin, you must detect his presence; and to detect his presence, you must differentiate yourself from him. On occasion his amorphous style of relating may make this a difficult task. It is, however, possible. One way to do this is to slow down and establish the current moment as a home base from which to witness your gremlin. I am about to describe two ways of doing this. I hope that you will experiment with these methods. Doing so will require your full attention and obviously you cannot be reading this book and giving your full attention to these methods at the same time. I suggest that you take a moment or two to read the next few pages and then when you are in a mood to experiment, do precisely what I suggest.

GUIDING YOUR AWARENESS

One way to establish the current moment as a vantage point from which to view your gremlin is by gently guiding your awareness back and forth from one area of awareness to another. The areas of awareness, again, are your body; the world as you experience it through your sensory receptors; and the world of make-believe.

First, focus your awareness on your breathing. Gently concentrate on a few breaths noticing the movement of the air through your nose, down your trachea and into your lungs. Pay very close attention to the movement of your abdomen as you breathe and to the movement of your chest as you take air in and blow it out. Make certain to draw into your lungs all of the air that you want. There is no need to hyperventilate or to breathe heavily. Simply take in all of the air that you want and when you exhale, exhale fully blowing out the last bit of air. Breathe at a pace that is comfortable for you. Your awareness may drift. It may go to your mental processes (the world of make-believe), to a sound outside of the room, or to an itch, or some other bodily sensation. It is natural for your awareness to wander; however, at the point you become aware that this is happening, consciously bring your awareness back to your breathing, tracing breaths in and out of your body. This is a very gentle process. It is not something you *try* to do. It is something you *allow* yourself to do. Be gentle with yourself. Do this for a minute or two. Go slow and relax. Once you are breathing comfortably, allow your awareness to focus on the surface of your skin. Your skin is a receptor. It is an organ and if you will attend to it you will be able to feel air on your skin, your clothes against your skin, and even perspiration and hair. For one or two minutes gently glide your awareness back and forth between your breathing and your skin.

Not only is your skin a very sensitive receptor, it is also a boundary. It separates you from all other matter in the universe. While this may seem too obvious to mention, I recommend that for a brief moment while noticing your breathing and your skin, that you attend to your physical separateness from

the world around you. Simply attend to your skin as a vibrating boundary between yourself and the rest of the world. Pay attention to your separateness from all else. You may experience a sense of being encased by your skin. It may be as if you are peering out from your body into a three-dimensional movie we will call "The World That Surrounds You." You may, at the same instant, be aware of your skin tingling and feeling very alive. I call this state of separateness "Being Grounded."

BEING GROUNDED

Being grounded is no better than not being grounded. It is simply a way of being. To opt for a basic here-and-now existential orientation to life might work very well for you. On the other hand, it might be boring and inconsistent with your natural style of being. For goodness sake do not give yourself some kind of rule in the form of "should" or "ought to" when it comes to being grounded. To tell yourself you should be grounded or ought to "be here now" is to set up a duality between your natural being and your gremlin. In order to become aware of your gremlin and to eventually tame him, however, it will behoove you to establish "being grounded" as a home base that you can return to at will. "Being grounded" can become a powerful reference point from which to focus your awareness on your body, on the world around you via your sensory receptors, or on the world of make-believe.

NOW I AM AWARE

Another method of grounding yourself is to play a simple game entitled: "Now I Am Aware Of." Using one sense at a time and going slowly, simply focus your awareness on one aspect of your environment after another. Take the time to really notice whatever you bring into your field of awareness be it a sound, a sight, a smell, something you touch, or something you taste. Go slow. As you gain relaxed control of your awareness you may want to experiment with channeling it from your body—to the world around you—to the world of make-believe, staying a few seconds in each place. As thoughts come into your awareness, simply notice them and let them go. Gently channel your awareness back inside or outside beginning phrases with "Now I am aware of..." As for me:

> "Now I am aware of the sound of the pencil
>   lead on the paper;
> Now I hear music in the background;
> Now I am aware of the breeze on my skin;
> Now I am aware of thinking about what
>   to write;
> Now I am aware of a tightness around
>   my eyes."

Your gremlin will want you to spend no time at all going slowly and increasing your awareness. He knows the power of simply noticing as a tool for taming him and it frightens him. He will do his best to distract you. Listen to his monologue. It may sound like scolding or disoriented jabber, like advice from a true friend, or even like interesting intellectual pontification. In any event, it is your gremlin. Simply notice him without allowing yourself to become involved with him. If you find yourself involved, simply channel your

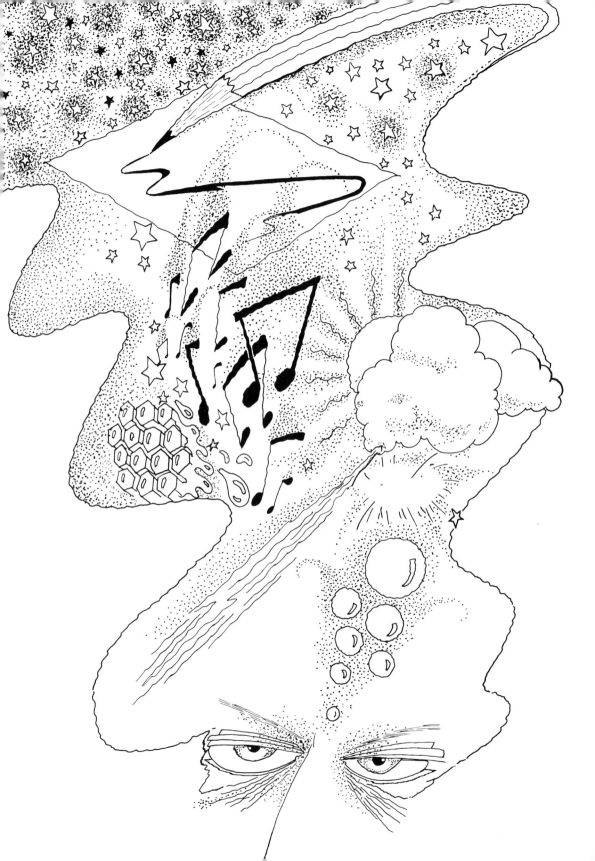

awareness back to your body or the world around you using the words "Now I am aware..."

Until now, observing your gremlin has been difficult because of the enmeshed quality of your relationship with him. However, as you increase your ability to ground yourself, you will begin to detach yourself from your gremlin. From a position of being grounded, you can observe him. You probably won't be able to hear his voice, but you will be able to experience it and to make some statements about its speed, volume, rhythm, and its intensity. If you relax, you may even experience certain colors that seem to go with your gremlin. You may experience his size, or his shape. Again, becoming aware of your gremlin is not something that requires intellectual knowledge, strain, study or even intense concentration. It involves only relaxing and *simply noticing*. It is something you allow yourself to do, not something you *try* to do. If you begin to have a clear experience of your gremlin, you might want to jot down some words that describe him. You might even want to sketch a picture of him on the note paper at the end of the book. Chances are by the time you have finished this book you will have more than one picture; for remember, gremlins change their style of being regularly. Yours may have a very distinct look on occasion, and at other times be rather vague. He may be large or small, human or inhuman, colorful or bland. From your vantage point of being grounded you will now be able to observe him. As you observe him you will become aware of some of the habits and concepts he uses to stifle your enjoyment. We are about to spend some time refining our abilities to simply notice these. Our primary tool will be awareness. Remember that taming your gremlin involves simply noticing; being at choice and playing with options; and being in process.

AWARENESS OF HABITS

Your gremlin has trapped you into forming habits for leading life. These habits fall into two general categories:

Habits for responding to
feelings.

Habits for responding to
people.

Habits for
Responding to Feelings

There is a difference between feeling and thinking. Feelings are physical sensations not mental processes. Feelings make themselves known in your body. Thoughts occur in the world of make-believe. Feelings fall into four basic categories: anger, sadness, joy, and sexual feeling. When one of these feelings is conjured up, your response may be a habitual one based on a belief rooted in the past. For example, if you learned from experience or from being told that anger is hurtful and its expression evil, your habit may be to block your anger. The same may be true if you equate sadness with weakness, sex with sin, or joy with immaturity. It is difficult to become aware of your habits because you are (to borrow an old adage) "too close to the forest to see the trees." It is almost as if you are *of* your habits — until, that is, you begin to "simply notice" them. As you begin to gently regulate the flow of your awareness from your body —

to the world around you—to the world of make-believe, your habits will become more and more obvious to you. You may notice, for example, that your physical response to anger is to habitually shorten your breathing. Your behavioral response may be to talk yourself out of your anger, to rationalize it, to rant and rave, to eat, to drink, or to fight. You may experience anger as powerful, as sexy, as scary, or as disgusting. You might become energized by anger, nauseous, vengeful, super-nice, sarcastic, placating, attacking, very analytical; or you might go to outrageous lengths to avoid the feeling. I hope that beginning today you will pay close attention to your habitual responses to anger keeping in mind that your anger may, at times, take the form of a minor irritation and at other times you may experience it as a tidal wave of rage. Don't analyze your feeling however you experience it. Simply notice it. Notice the effect of anger on your body; especially on your breathing. When you choose not to express it, what do you do with it instead? You may find that you store it in your stomach, your neck, your shoulders, your head, or your back. I'm certainly not suggesting that you should always *express* your anger. I am suggesting only that you *simply notice* your habits for responding to this emotion. Are you more comfortable expressing anger with men; women; young people; old people? What happens to your voice when you get angry? Simply notice.

The following experiment may help you get a handle on some of your beliefs about the nature of anger. It is on these beliefs that your habits are based. Read the following items in a state of relaxed concentration, and allow yourself to honestly fill in the blanks with your reactions. If you need more space, use the note paper in the back of this book.

1. A time I really felt angry at another human

being was _____

_____

2. At that time I chose to_____

_____

3. As I remember that experience now I feel

_____

_____

4. If I had allowed my anger to be reflected in
my body and in my voice in a manner that
was absolutely uncensored, I imagine that

I would have _____

_____

5. The angriest that I ever recall seeing anybody

be was _____

_____

6. When I witnessed him or her being that angry,

I felt _____

_____

7. When my mother was angry, she tended to

_____

_____

8. When my father was angry, he tended to

_____

_____

9. It seems to me that I automatically associate anger with (choose all that apply):
   a) power
   b) good
   c) bad
   d) productivity
   e) masculinity
   f) pain
   g) aliveness
   h) excitement
   i) darkness
   j) creativity
   k) harm

add your own responses:

   l) _____

   m) _____

I hope that you have been honest with yourself and that you have done the above experiment in a state of relaxed concentration. Your gremlin will not like this sort of awareness activity and will encourage you to leave well-enough alone. He wants you to lead your life out of habit for he knows that this will lead you to an eventual feeling of emptiness.

Look over your responses to the above items. Perhaps you can glean from them a clue or two relevant to your habitual response(s) to anger. There is no need for you to be frightened or cautious about acknowledging your beliefs and/or habits. Doing so does not imply that you need to change anything. If you become aware of beliefs or habits relevant to your reaction to anger, you may wish to jot them down on the paper in the back of this book. Think through the validity of these beliefs or habits for you at this stage of your life, remembering that a habitual response, which made sense when it was formed, may have little value in your life as you currently experience it

Now what about sadness, sexual feeling, joy? Yes, joy.

I meet people frequently who implode joy. I love the pictures of Charles Schulz's Snoopy doing his supper-time dance. Such open joy is a beautiful thing. But some folks confuse joy with silliness, irresponsibility, immaturity, and being out of control. Such notions are the tools of your gremlin. Simply notice your responses to joy and happiness in the next few weeks. Don't try to change; just notice your habitual responses. You may even hear your gremlin whispering or yelling to you his rationale for having you keep the lid on your full experience of joy. If so, simply notice him.

And as for your sadness, did you know that a full experience of sadness can feel invigorating? Many people confuse sadness with depression. Actually, sadness and depression are very different experiences. Sadness is a natural response to certain stimuli. It often results in tears and full breathing. It can be a full, rich feeling. Depression, on the other hand, is the result of blocking sadness, or of blocking anger. Depression is what can happen when our gremlin convinces us that our feelings are unacceptable. When we are depressed, we have a sense of being deadened and blocked. When we fully experience our sadness, we may not feel on top of the world, but we will feel very much alive and may even have a sense of well-being. Most importantly, when we experience our feelings fully, we will eventually move through them to a new feeling space. On the other hand, if we avoid our feelings, we tend to stick ourselves in a particular emotional state.

What do you habitually do with your sadness? Remember a time when you felt sad, over a loss, perhaps, or in a sad movie. How did you react? Did your gremlin convince you to legislate against your sadness? If so, you probably started breathing rather shallowly and developed a tight, full feeling in your throat, or a headache. That was your choice and in some instances it may be better to suffer these physical sensations than to cry. To start bawling at a time when the repercussions would cause you pain or embarrassment wouldn't do much to help you enjoy yourself. Remember, the key here is to operate out of choice rather than out of habit. What you do with

Take this ol' familiar road...

WARNING

DETOUR

your sadness is for you to decide; not once and for all, but on each occasion in which your sadness emerges. There is, however, value in observing your habits for responding to anger and to sadness, as it is operating out of habit that your gremlin will use to lead you into a state of misery.

Let's talk about sexual feeling for a few moments. Notice what you do when you feel sexy and turned-on. Sure, it depends on the circumstances, but has your gremlin convinced you to respond to sexual feelings out of habit? I have met men whose gremlins had them convinced that ejaculation was a necessary response to getting an erection. And I have met men and women whose gremlins had convinced them that sexual feeling was lust and that lust was sinful. What about you? Notice your habitual responses to sexual feeling. Do your habits vary from circumstance to circumstance? What does feeling sexy feel like to you? Do you feel weak, strong, wet, warm, angry, anxious, electrified, loving? Notice over the next few weeks. Just relax and observe. Whatever you notice is fine. Relax and pay attention.

Your gremlin may be afraid of what you and I are doing here. He may make an intense effort to convince you that this is unnecessary and unproductive. Simply listen to his chatter remembering that it is just useless noise. If you become aware of doubts or second thoughts about reading further, simply notice them and either go on reading or stop for a while. You might want to jot down your gremlin's words. Simply notice his objections. For goodness sake, don't haggle with him or upset yourself.

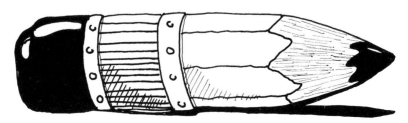

Habits for
Responding to People

You probably have developed habits for how to respond to people with particular characteristics. Your gremlin has helped you to establish these habits and wants you to lead your life in accordance with them. You may be bound and determined not to be judgmental, and the idea of stereotyping people may be repugnant to your nature. Unfortunately, your gremlin loves the idea. He knows that clouding your actual experience with preconceived notions will keep you from experiencing the excitement of the current moment and he is well aware that excitement is a prerequisite for enjoying this life. As you become more and more familiar with your gremlin you will notice also that he has convinced you to adopt habits for responding certain ways in certain situations. You may, for example behave in the same general way whenever you meet with authority figures, or with people with gray hair, or on first dates. You may tend to repeat the same general behaviors over and over in like situation after like situation. These habits are neither good nor bad, however they may be based on the world as you perceived it at some other point in time. Habits that you learned long ago may still be suitable and effective, however they may also be antiquated and limit your enjoyment of your existence. After all, the world for you as an adult is far different from the world for you as a child, or even for you a few years ago. What worked for you in past years may not work well for you now. *As long as you operate out of habit you will limit your ability to enjoy yourself.*

By acting out of habit, you will replay the same life dramas over and over again. The characters and settings may vary but the outcome generally will be the same. Your gremlin will (sometimes very subtly) convince you that operating out of habit is for your own safety. Notice, however, that if you opt for your habitual patterns time after time, you will begin to feel blah, bored, discontent, possibly depressed, and eventually empty. Gremlins love emptiness; for you cannot enjoy yourself and feel empty at the same time.

FEAR

Habits are cemented in place by fear. Fear is your gremlin's primary tool. At the time he talked you into forming a particular behavior into a habit, that behavior may have made very good sense. If, as a child, when you expressed anger or discontent your parents punished you, it would have made sense for you to develop a "happy face facade." (One of my least favorite facades. People who truly enjoy themselves don't feel the need to smile all the time.) A behavior that you incorporated as a child may still be appropriate in certain situations. To the extent that that behavior is a habit, however, it will interfere with your excitement, your spontaneity, and your potential for creative living. In short, the quality of your life will be dramatically affected.

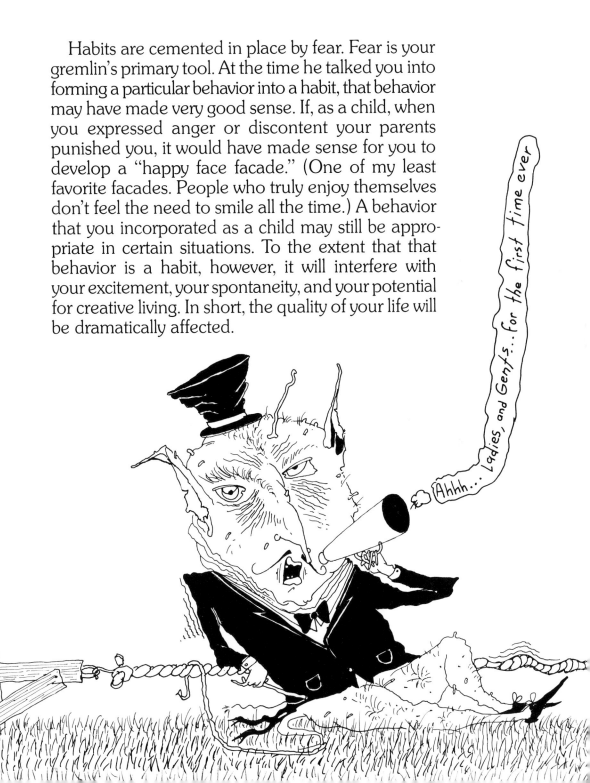

Gremlins I have known have created very personalized, fear-inducing, catastrophic expectations for the purpose of taunting the souls on which they labor. Some of the lines used by gremlins I've met have included:

If you risk changing, you will:

> lose friends
> fail
> be wrong
> be poor
> be rejected
> be embarrassed

and many, many more. Scrutinized closely, these fears are but honey-coated derivatives of a very, very ominous and powerful gremlin myth: *IF YOU DO NOT DO THINGS HIS WAY YOU WILL END UP ALONE AND/OR IN SEVERE PHYSICAL OR EMOTIONAL PAIN AND/OR DEAD.* Your gremlin is not the cute little character he may at first appear to be. He is not fooling around. Remember the good news, however. You can render him entirely impotent if you will:

> SIMPLY NOTICE;
>
> CHOOSE AND PLAY WITH OPTIONS;
>
> and
>
> BE IN PROCESS.

I hope that you will not give yourself the rule that you should change old habits. A new rule implies no more than a new habit. Adopt a spirit of adventure. Experiment with change ONCE IN A WHILE. Change for a change. Enjoy yourself. Later we will talk more about the art of playing with options and being in process.

AWARENESS OF CONCEPTS

Any concept is false. Let us take your self-concept, for example.

Your Self-Concept

Your self-concept is faulty for one simple reason: you are not a concept. I meet people frequently who are unhappy because they are not living up to their concept of who they are or of who they imagine they are supposed to be. Some judge themselves as too passive, others as too sad, others as too greedy, and on and on. I even meet people who are so unhappy with who they think they are that they try to do away with themselves. Sometimes they try this physically and other times by creating new concepts of how and whom they want to be. I have met people who try to fit themselves into one self-concept after another. This is a sure-fire way to become miserable. Breaking through concepts is a very powerful tool when it comes to taming your gremlin. In my work with whole families I have noticed that personal growth and enjoyment begin emerging rapidly once family members begin to recognize that their style of being together does not have to approximate the style of any other family on the planet. At the point family members begin to clearly see the rigidity of their concepts and expectations regarding themselves, one another, and their family as a unit, the fun begins. They are then free to go about tapping their creativity toward the goal of developing a harmonious mini-society suited to their *particular* desires and personalities. The same is true for individuals. At the point an individual becomes excited about who he or she actually is rather than who he wants to convince himself he is, enjoyment becomes much more attainable.

ENJOYING YOURSELF HAS MORE TO DO WITH ACTUALIZING YOUR SELF THAN WITH ACTUALIZING YOUR CONCEPT OF WHO YOU IMAGINE YOU ARE SUPPOSED TO BE.

That is to say, enjoying yourself is not the same as "getting your act together." Feeling good is a product of becoming aware of who you are beneath your act or acts.

Acts

We are all, to some extent, actors. We act in order to get what we imagine we need from the world. Our acts are often the result of the fears our gremlin has instilled in us. They are very personal in that they incorporate our habits and concepts in all of their complexity. As you become aware of the personal acts you have created, you will become aware, also, that you have created an imaginary audience. In your audience, sitting front row center, will be your most powerful critic—your gremlin. He may represent a composite of the value judgments made by other people in your imaginary audience. Your audience may include your mother, father, boss, friends, enemies, colleagues, someone with whom you feel or felt competitive, in short—those whom you allow to have influence over your actions and feelings. At times you will receive critics' acclaim and audience applause. As a result you will feel very good. At other times the response of your critics will leave you discouraged. Even if you become a very fine actor, you will notice that you feel empty much of the time; for you will realize that the critics' acclaim and the loud applause from your audience are offered in response to your act, rather than to the real you. You may create a facade that will be very well liked. You may have one or more very good acts that are even loved; but what of the real you that is inside and behind the act? Are you ever seen, heard, or touched? A good act may get you what you want for a while — the critics' acclaim I mentioned earlier, high self-esteem, a few strokes, even money. For this reason I have devoted the last section of this book to developing your act. At this time, however, let me simply remind you that you are *not* your act and that shifting from one act to another does not imply qualitative personal growth or increased comfort with yourself.

To Be or NOT to Be... To Be... To Do... Do Be... Do Be.. Do be.. Do wah.. Oowah...

You Are Not Your Act

Among the acts I have seen in recent years are: super-executive, back-to-the-land-woodsman, discotheque hot mamma (and poppa), urban cowboy, alcoholic, religious zealot, music groupie, personal growth groupie, helpless-dependent woman, assertive "new" woman, macho man, and sensitive male. Some people blend several acts very, very well. At this point, I would like you to be honest with yourself. You might ask yourself what your best act is. Have you more than one? A good way to get into your act(s) is to jot down a few words reflective of how you want to be seen by the people you most want to impress. Ask yourself what your considerations are as you stand in front of your closet selecting clothes to wear. Early in your relationships with people what do you let them know about you either by virtue of how you behave or by virtue of what you tell them? What would you most like them to say about you if you weren't around? You might enjoy jotting down your responses to some of these items. Don't be embarrassed. Remember, you have developed your act(s) for perfectly logical reasons. You developed them to get you what you wanted, and probably what you believed you needed. Your act may work superbly or it may be dismally ineffective. The important task is to recognize that an act is an act and not to confuse it with the real you.

Some of my clients have even named their more
familiar acts. They seldom use them now and certainly
they are clear that they are not their acts. In recent
months I have met Lash LaRue, The Red Queen,
Little Miss What-The-Hell, Peace-Love-Dove-Sigh-
Blissed-Out-Earth-Mother, Muscles, Laid-Back
Brother, and many others. Acting can be fun. There
is nothing wrong with developing an act; however, to

let your gremlin delude you into thinking that you are or should be your act will result in your feeling anxious and empty during the times you perform your act poorly. The hard truth is that your act is just as transparent as everyone else's. Sooner or later you will disappoint your gremlin and those whose applause you seek. When you do, you will not enjoy yourself and to not enjoy yourself is a drag.

A Word About
Acts and Relationships

I counsel many people who are involved in relationships that are important to them. I have noticed that often relationships begin with a covert agreement between two people that sounds something like this:

> "I promise to help you convince yourself that you are the way you want to think you are, if you will promise to do the same for me."

Actors and actresses tend to seek each other out and perform plays together. They never say aloud that this is what they are doing, but it is. I have seen several variations of the "Knight in Shining Armor Meets Damsel in Distress" theme. The first scene is often terrific, but the whole thing begins to get unpleasantly intense when one or the other gets tired of acting or sees through the other's act. When this happens there is often disappointment, resentment, and defensiveness about the deterioration of one's own act or the act of his or her own partner. At this stage of the game there is the potential for a great deal of conflict. Both parties' gremlins will come charging in full force supporting those ugly fears of abandonment, pain, and death I spoke of earlier. The gremlin's monologue may have a defensive flavor:

> "S/he's holding you back."
> "S/he is too difficult to please."
> "S/he is unreasonable."
> "S/he is no longer the person you married."
> "S/he doesn't give you the emotional support you need."
> "S/he's too independent."

or a self-critical tone:

> "S/he deserves more than you can give him/her."
> "You're so dumb."
> "You should be stronger."
> "You should be less selfish."
> "You'll never amount to anything."
> "He deserves more than I can give him."

The up side is that within all of this sticky intensity is a wonderful opportunity for two people to see their acts as mere acts, and to begin to establish a relationship based on a mutual desire to be intimate and enjoy themselves. Intimacy requires the ability to share your true self with another and to experience his or her true self. You cannot be intimate with another so long as your pure contact with him or her is interfered with by your act. Allowing the real you to emerge and be experienced by another involves allowing your body, your voice, your facial expressions, and your words to express you rather than your act or self-concept, or your habits. Removing these barriers leaves you exposed (which may be scary) and available for love and enjoyment (which is exciting). Excitement almost always underlies fear, and excitement is a prerequisite to enjoying yourself.

Concepts of 'What Is So'

You probably hold concepts not only of yourself but of other people, things, processes, and relationships. It is valuable in taming your gremlin to know the difference between concepts and the things concepts represent. Simply put: "The word is not the thing, nor the description the described." Even more simply put, and you needn't applaud my originality,

"There is no substitute for experience." If your mouth were dry and your throat were parched, I could say the word "water" to you for eons and your mouth would stay dry and your throat would stay parched. I could read you Webster's definition of water and still you would be thirsty. I could even describe to you water's physical properties and still your thirst would remain unquenched. But one small taste of the actual thing called "water" will aid in relieving your thirst even if you are unable to spell the word "water," much less define it. This same analogy holds true for every object, process, and relationship, and it has relevance to the process of taming your gremlin. As you improve your ability to gently channel your awareness and as you continue to practice doing so, you will become increasingly conscious of your gremlin and his use of concepts. Concepts are like a veil between your essence and the world as it actually exists. That is why your gremlin uses them. Direct contact with your environment leads to excitement and excitement is a prerequisite for enjoying yourself. Lack of contact will, over time, lead to boredom and boredom is no more than a form of deadening. If you allow your gremlin to deaden you by having you see the world through a veil of concepts, you will miss out on the excitement of direct experience. Without excitement you will begin to live a less than vibrant life and eventually you will feel very, very empty. In short, you will not enjoy yourself.

As you begin to differentiate yourself from your gremlin you will find it easier and easier to simply notice your concepts. For goodness sake don't *try* to rid yourself of them or to argue them out with your gremlin. Grappling with your gremlin is often a mistake, even if your grappling is over the validity of a habit or concept, or an attempt to resolve an emotional dilemma.

GRAPPLING WITH YOUR GREMLIN

Your gremlin wants you to believe that if you go over and over the facts and factors surrounding an uncomfortable set of emotions, you will eventually figure your way out of the discomfort. He prefers you to "think about" rather than to "experience." He is afraid to have you fully experience the basic emotions we have mentioned of anger, sadness, sexual feeling, and joy, and he is equally afraid of their derivatives such as irritability, depression, and embarrassment. He knows that when you are experiencing your feelings your awareness is on you rather than on him, and when your awareness is not on him, he has no effect on you. He knows also that if you fully experience your uncomfortable feelings you will eventually move through them to a point of resolution and enjoyment. Becoming involved in intellectual discussions and arguments with your gremlin is to pay your gremlin far too much attention. This is a dangerous mistake. Your gremlin is to you as the tar baby was to Br'er Rabbit. He wants you to become involved with him, but every degree of involvement leads to more involvement. Your gremlin is a sticky sort and the more you fight with him the more enmeshed you will become in his depressive muck. If you grapple with your gremlin, you will eventually become anxious, frustrated, and tired of the whole issue at hand (regardless of the issue). You will want to let go of the issue and drop the whole subject, but you will be trapped. Your gremlin will lead you to believe that if you continue to analyze the issue, you will eventually figure your way out of the entire entanglement. Your gremlin is cruel. A quick and common example of how grappling with your gremlin can get you into trouble is one having to do with jealousy.

In my experience counseling couples, I have encountered hundreds of jealous husbands and wives. Jealousy, like any human process, is neither innately good nor innately bad. If, however, the only payoff for jealousy is misery for the people involved, it really doesn't make much sense, now does it? Especially if one's goal is to feel good—to enjoy oneself. Many of the jealous people I see are uncomfortable with their jealousy on one level, but stimulated by it on the other.

I saw a couple recently who loved one another very much. Let's call them John and Sarah. John was very upset, almost in anguish, because his wife told him that she found one of their mutual male friends "sexy." That is all she said. The comment seemed like an innocent one, even to John. But John's gremlin took hold and invited him into the world of make-believe. In the world of make-believe, he tortured John with quick fleeting fantasies of his wife making love with the man, his wife leaving him (John), and his wife being more attracted to the "other man" than to him. As he really began to open up to me, he shared that on occasion he fantasized catching his wife in a romantic encounter with the man and eventually he realized and shared with me that he found the whole idea somehow stimulating. It didn't make him happy, but it stimulated him — sort of like picking a sore. And that is how it is with gremlins. They do their best to convince us to settle for titillation rather than for full, rich fulfillment and happiness. The point I am trying to make here is that John could have wondered for days about his wife and her intentions (as a matter of fact, he did). In one of our conjoint sessions, he even talked with her about his feelings, and he shared his fears and fantasies. She gave him all of the reassurance one person could give another and intellectually he believed her. However, in the days that followed, his gremlin persisted in reintroducing the disturbing questions and fantasies. John tried over and over to work the issue out in his head and he discussed the matter several times with his wife. On occasion he would convince himself of his wife's fidelity. He could see the misery that he was perpetuating in himself and between the two of them. It was as if they were both sick and tired of the whole issue but John felt compelled to think about it. He grew irritable with Sarah and their discussions about the matter began to feel like interrogations to her. John knew that what he was doing was no good for their relationship, but he felt like he couldn't leave the whole matter alone. In one of our sessions he likened his experience to that of watching a sexy, slightly violent movie. He didn't have loving feelings while going over the confused morass of facts and fantasies his gremlin dangled before him, but he was stimulated.

Your gremlin knows precisely how to get your attention and he will create movies in your head suited to your vulnerabilities. They may be sexy, sad, violent, or scary, or like beautiful fairy tales, but certainly they will be suited to drawing and holding your attention. You will find yourself dying to know the ending of the movie and forget that the only real ending is to leave the theater or to not take the movie so seriously (after all, it is just a movie).

The problem in this whole scenario was not Sarah's relationship to a sexy man, or even John's relationship to Sarah. The toxic relationship at play here was the one between John and his gremlin. John was giving his gremlin far too much attention. Instead of simply noticing and hearing his chatter, he was seriously considering what the gremlin had to say and hoping to disprove it. He was grappling with his gremlin. John continually went over and over the facts, fantasies, and questions raised by his gremlin hoping to think the whole matter out to a peaceful, all-conclusive, ever-lasting resolution. A far better method would have been to use the first step of our gremlin taming scheme, that is, to breathe, relax, and simply notice his gremlin without becoming involved with him. He might have even chosen to grapple with his gremlin for a while. The key word here is "chosen."

Choosing to grapple with your gremlin is far different from being unconsciously sucked into participating in a misery-making wrestling match with him. When you grapple by *choice*, you retain some control of the grappling. Even with choice, to grapple with your gremlin is always a bit risky. Gremlins are tenacious and once they have you involved with them it is difficult to escape. For this reason I recommend that when you choose to grapple with your gremlin, you do so only for a few seconds or moments at a time and only after setting a very precise time limit on your grappling. Make certain to stop at the end of the time period. One to ten minutes is usually more than enough grappling time. Having set the time limit ahead of time, you can get in there and grapple to your heart's delight. Have a ball—fantasize, analyze, ruminate, obsess, get turned on, be violent, miserable, happy, wretched, down, up, whatever—*for a few minutes*. Then stop and ground yourself.

Your gremlin is proficient at creating a cerebral house of mirrors. Even if on some rare occasion you manage to arrange the concepts in your head in such a way that you feel like the intellectual victor over your gremlin, it will not last. Within a few minutes, or at best a few days, he will raise the whole issue again and you will find yourself struggling with intense desperation to resolve the whole matter from start to finish. Taming your gremlin has absolutely nothing to do with out-arguing him or with being right. Remember also that taming your gremlin has nothing to do with trying and straining. It has to do with simply noticing; choosing and playing with options; and being in process.

AN AGE-OLD THEORY
OF GREMLIN TAMING

As you directly experience how you are or who you are, your gremlin's myths, the habits he has talked you into accepting, and the concepts he is perpetuating, there will occur an automatic adjustment upward in your enjoyment level. Why this is so I don't know, but it is so and it has been so forever. Some call this phenomena "the existential theory of change," some call it "the Gestalt theory of change," some call it "the paradoxical theory of change," some call it "the Zen theory of change." Simply stated it reads something like this:

I CHANGE NOT BY TRYING TO BE
SOMETHING OTHER THAN I AM.
I CHANGE BY BEING
FULLY AWARE OF HOW I AM.

When you try to become something other than you are the best you can do is develop an act. When you develop an act, you place yourself in the position of the performer we discussed earlier and you place your gremlin in the position of critic. The gratification that comes even from the greatest of performances is short-lived. On the other hand, when you initiate the business of actualizing *yourself* instead of your act, you begin to feel better automatically. Four thousand years ago, Lao Tzu wrote:

> "Notice the natural order of things. Work with it rather than against it for to try to change what is so will only set up resistance."

Lao Tzu was a smart cookie.

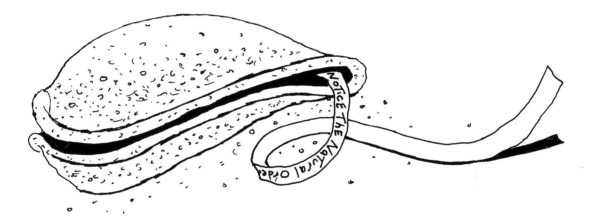

AN EXERCISE

Completing the exercise that follows may be helpful in clueing you as to some of the habits and concepts your gremlin may be using to confine you. Simply relax, breathe, and enjoy yourself while you play within the context of the following experiment. It is unnecessary to work at it or to strain.

Allow yourself to remember, for a moment, a house in which you lived between the ages of 3 and 7. If you lived in more than one house during this time, choose the one that you have the warmest feeling about. On the blank paper that I've included, create a house-plan style drawing of the house (as if you were above the house looking down). If phrases such as "I'm a terrible artist" or "I hate to draw" fly through your head, notice them and then let them go. These are concepts your gremlin is feeding you. He's tricky. Simply relax and sketch the house as you remember it. For goodness sake, don't worry about being exact with regard to proportions or layout. Here, as an example, is a drawing of the house I grew up in:

Now, just for a moment, allow yourself to reflect on each room in the house. Jot down key words and draw symbols in each room relevant to your memories of being in that room. Remember that these need make sense to no one but you, and remember also that there is absolutely no way to do this wrong. Enjoy yourself. You may be surprised at how much or how little you remember. You may recall pictures that hung on the wall; a design on the floor tile or carpeting; furniture; even molding around doors. How much or how little you remember is of no real importance. It is no better to recall lots of details than to recall only a few details. This is not a test, it is an exercise and it is being offered to you in the interest of self-exploration and enjoyment. Relax. Go slow. Allow yourself to remember each room. You may recall a certain smell, a general feeling, or even a color associated with a given room and probably you will become aware of variations in your general sense as you let your awareness move along from room to room. Simply notice your feelings and thoughts as you do this, jotting down a few words or symbols as reminders of your memories. As for me: At this moment, I am remembering the feeling of lying next to my father in my parents'bedroom. We were listening to a boxing match. I remember how good he smelled and how warm his flannel pajamas were as I lay next to him. I remember that Ezzard Charles was boxing. I don't know that I ever thought about the experience before, but at this moment it seems that it was extremely pleasurable. I was very happy there next to him.

While living in this house you had a vast number of experiences and from these experiences you probably formed many ideas about yourself, about relationships, and about the nature of existence. Learning that occurs experientially is very deep-seated. It is as if the learning is in our bones rather than simply in our intellect. Often our experiential learnings and the beliefs we form as a result are outside of our awareness. They are so much a part of us that to step back and objectively view them is difficult. Yet, they affect us day in and day out from situation to situation.

In order to become a bit more aware of beliefs and habits you may have formed while living in this house, I have included below some items to which you can respond. Relax as you read each item and be honest with yourself. The sort of concentration involved in this experience is akin to that required for watching a movie. You don't have to furrow your brow or strain in order to get into it; yet you have to pay attention in order to enjoy yourself. This is the sort of "effortless effort" I am asking of you. Respond to these items based on what you saw and heard, not on what you were told.

From what you experienced in this house, what did you learn about:
the expression of love _____

_____

physical stroking such as hugging and kissing _____

_____

causing people physical pain _____

_____

how family decisions are made _____

_____

the expression of sadness _____

_____

the expression of joy _____

_____

trust _____

_____

honesty _____

_____

how men are _____

_____

how women are _____

_____

how smart you are _____

_____

how capable a leader you are _____

_____

about your athletic abilities _____

_____

your creative abilities_____

_____

how lovable you are_____

_____

how likeable you are_____

_____

how sexy you are_____

_____

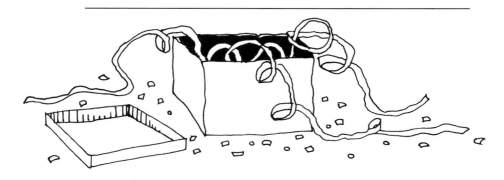

Look back over your responses to these items and consider them as representative of a few of the concepts you have tended to lead your life in accordance with. As you look at each of these learnings, you might ask yourself, "Does this learning have value in my life today? Does it take into account who I am today? Is this learning something that I have altered over time? Is this learning something that I wish to reconsider from this point forward?"

As you move through the world from this day forth, you will have an ongoing opportunity to observe your concepts and your habits for responding to feelings and to people. If you notice yourself operating out of habit, consider the possibility that your gremlin is on the scene. Remember, habits and concepts are not awful and I certainly hope you won't give yourself the message that you should modify every habit or concept. What is important when it comes to gremlin taming is to relax and breathe and to: simply notice; choose and play with options; and be in process.

REALITY AND DUALITY

Your gremlin will insist that your habits and the concepts on which your habits are based are necessary to your well-being. He may insist by kicking you in the head and making demands, by frightening you with catastrophic expectations of the future, by reminding you of the nasty consequences of your acts in past situations where you did not listen to him, and even by gently putting his arm around you and convincing you that he has your best interest at heart. Regardless of how he presents himself he is your gremlin and his view of "what is so" is grounded in make-believe. Be aware of him. It is unnecessary to *try* to ignore him or to fight. Simply notice him. From your vantage point of being grounded you will be able to hear his chatter. Listen to it, think of it as just chatter. Remember — to fight with your gremlin is to lose to your gremlin. At the point you begin fighting with your gremlin you are in a state of duality.

Taming your gremlin involves being in reality not in duality. When you are in reality, your energy flows freely within you and is available to you for your use in relating to the world. Here is a simple conceptuali-zation of a person feeling whole and in reality rather than in duality.

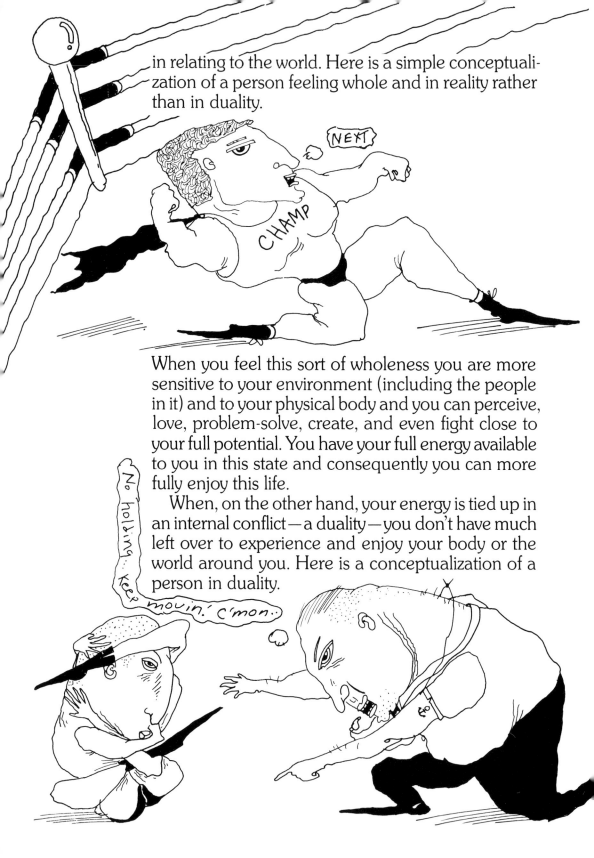

When you feel this sort of wholeness you are more sensitive to your environment (including the people in it) and to your physical body and you can perceive, love, problem-solve, create, and even fight close to your full potential. You have your full energy available to you in this state and consequently you can more fully enjoy this life.

When, on the other hand, your energy is tied up in an internal conflict—a duality—you don't have much left over to experience and enjoy your body or the world around you. Here is a conceptualization of a person in duality.

In this state of being you will feel anxious and/or disgruntled and/or bottled-up and/or empty. In short—you will not enjoy yourself. Your gremlin prefers you to stay in a state of duality.

Let me remind you to do yourself a favor and simply read and enjoy this book. Do not, I repeat, do not try and figure out anything. The *real you* understands what you have read. No analysis is necessary. Relax and breathe. If you get bored and frustrated, stop for a while.

If your gremlin wants you to listen to him, you might even write down some of his words on some of the note paper in the back of the book.

TIPS FOR DETECTING YOUR GREMLIN

An undetected gremlin can create asthma, heart attacks, ulcers, colitis, headaches, backaches, neuroses, psychoses, and just about any other sort of ailment you can imagine. You, however, have nothing to worry about so long as you are able to simply notice him. Be very specific about noticing any tension in your body for this will clue you to your gremlin's presence. If, for example, you notice that your breathing is shallow, pay attention to exactly how shallow it is. If your neck is tight, what muscles does the tightness cover? How tight is your neck? If you have a headache, how deep into your skull does the pain go? What are the parameters of the pain? Can you imagine a color of the pain? What might the color be? Simply notice your body and the effect of your gremlin on it. These effects will become more and more evident as will your gremlin himself. Analysis, judgment, and attempts to change are unnecessary.

When your gremlin is really working on you, he will shadow you to such an extent it will be as if you are absorbed by him. During these times it is as if you become him, and as your gremlin, you will feel self-righteous, defensive, greedy, and even down-right mean. Your attitude toward others will be defensive and manipulative. You will have an inordinate invest-

ment in making certain you are not taken advantage of. You might even consider throwing out this book. Your body may feel tight and this tension may manifest itself in a furrowed brow, a headache, upset stomach, or simply a mild tension. Your thoughts may become extremely rapid. The power with which your gremlin will be attempting to squelch your essence may be so intense that you will not even notice him unless you allow yourself the sort of self-awareness we practiced earlier. Use what you have learned about grounding yourself. Remember the key points I mentioned previously: to focus on your breathing for a few breaths; then to gently guide your awareness to the surface of your skin. Allow yourself the opportunity to become very aware of your skin as both a receptor and an encasement. As quickly as possible, gain the sense of being encased in your skin and peering out. Relax and return to your home base—the state of BEING GROUNDED.

For the next few days, you might want to pay attention to precisely how the following emotions in varying degrees of intensity affect your body: anger, sadness, joy, and sexual feelings. On the note paper I have provided, make notes of your physical reactions to your emotions. Pay special attention to the effects these emotions have on your breathing. You may choose, also, to key in on the parts of your body in which tension makes itself known. Notice your jaws, your head, your genitals, your stomach, the upper part of your back and your lower back. Notice your habits on both a physical and on a behavioral level. While it is counterproductive to *force* yourself to change a habit or concept in order to increase your level of enjoyment, it will expedite the process if you experiment with change *once in a while*, just for the fun of it. *Play* with options.

CHOOSING AND PLAYING
WITH OPTIONS

I want to emphasize the word "playing" in "playing with options." Playing implies enjoying yourself and that is precisely what I mean here. Experimenting with change can be scary. When you change a habitual way of responding to feelings and life circumstances, you really won't know if you're going to get roses or rotten tomatoes. As I've mentioned, however, underneath your fear is probably excitement. If you can enjoy the excitement and unpredictability inherent in letting go of those habitual responses, your gremlin taming process will be a relatively smooth one. Enjoying the process is an integral part of taming your gremlin. Your gremlin would have you believe that feeling good requires working hard, straining, gutting-up, trying, analyzing, grunting, groaning, working things out, and most of all, worrying. The truth is there is no positive cause-effect correlation between the action implied by any of these terms and enjoying yourself. Your self-enjoyment will increase as you enhance your gremlin taming abilities; that is as you become more adept at simply noticing (your body, the world around you, your habits for responding to feelings and life circumstances, and your concepts); being at choice and playing with options; and being in process.

68

If you are aware of telling yourself you *should* change, your gremlin has got you buffaloed. "Should," "ought to," and "must" are gremlin terms that will dampen the pleasure of experimentation. Instead, simply "change for a change." Play around. As you become aware of an old habit, an outdated concept or a view that is based on the world of make-believe instead of reality, consider playing with changing a behavior. Change for the moment. To vow to change forever would be to do no more than to develop a new habit or a new act. Granted, it may be a more constructive habit or act than the one you were using before, but any habit or act limits your potential for living a creative, enjoyable life. Again, a key word here is CHOICE.

BEING AT CHOICE

To be at choice from situation to situation and from moment to moment is vitally important in taming your gremlin.

On occasion I have met people who have had a little counseling. A little counseling is like a little knowledge of karate: it can get you into bad trouble. Here is a common scenario: A woman goes into counseling and becomes aware of her life-long tendency to repress her anger. Her new-found awareness is so exciting that she develops a new rule. Instead of thinking that she should *not* show anger, she now believes with a great deal of fervor that she should *always* show her anger. She has developed what I call "A New Wave Neurosis" and is no better off than before. Her gremlin, waiting in the wings, will either continue to badger her about how awful her anger is or with a sudden shift in tactics, he will begin to berate her every time she is not totally honest with her feelings of anger, telling her that she *should* be. Remember:

IN TAMING YOUR GREMLIN DO NOT MAKE NEW RULES. INSTEAD, SIMPLY NOTICE; BE AT CHOICE AND PLAY WITH OPTIONS; AND BE IN PROCESS.

For example, if your gremlin has convinced you that certain of your feelings are dangerous or wrong; or that you're not entitled to them, you will feel panicky when they come up. If, on the other hand, your gremlin has convinced you that some powerful emotions are physically intolerable and will hurt you if you hold them in, he may encourage you to express them immediately and without respect for living things around you. You may feel better for the moment, but in the long run your gremlin will win by setting you up to feel anxious, guilty, isolated, or empty. Respect your gremlin's trickiness. A key word for taming him in this sort of situation is SLOW. If, instead of listening to your gremlin, you will simply breathe, feel the feelings, and let them circulate through your body, you will notice that feelings are simply energy and to experience energy can give you a vibrant feeling of aliveness. After all, feelings are intended to be felt and enjoyed and used to benefit your existence. Anger is not inherently evil; sadness does not automatically lead to depression; sexual feelings don't engender promiscuity; joy is not the same as irresponsible silliness; and fear does not connote cowardice. The only time that feelings become dangerous is when we bottle them up or discharge them impulsively without respect for other living things.

Not acknowledging and not expressing feelings does not make them go away. By the same token, it is unnecessary to outwardly express every emotion. As you begin to pay closer and closer attention to your emotions and to their effect on your body, you will notice that there is nothing in an emotion to be afraid of. It is only your gremlin who is afraid of your emotions for he knows that when you are experiencing your emotions you feel very much alive and that that feeling of aliveness is a large part of enjoying yourself. Your gremlin would prefer that you focus your attention on him instead of on your feelings. Often in what appears to be an intense emotional situation, if you will simply relax and take the time to feel your emotions, reminding yourself that you do not HAVE to do anything with them and that they are not dangerous, you will experience a sense of *relaxed power*. This sense has been described many ways including self-actualized, integrated, whole, happy, loving, centered, in high self-esteem, high, good, and hunky-dory. As you, over and over, take the time to simply experience the physical sensations known as emotions, you will actually begin to enjoy them. Choosing options for what to do with them will become easier and more enjoyable. It may even feel like an adventure. Again, one of the most commonly overlooked options is to simply breathe and enjoy what you are feeling.

OPTIONS FOR EXPRESSION

When you decide to outwardly express a particular feeling it makes sense for you to select an option for doing so that leaves you feeling good on the inside and at the same time gets you what you want from the environment. The process for selecting these kinds of options is what makes taming your gremlin exciting, for here is where you can be creative. You will be surprised at the options you can think of for expressing yourself once you get into playing. On occasion you might select options that are consistent with your personality. At other times, you might select options that are totally out of character for you. So what? Be out of character. Being out of character might help you blow your act, and by now you recognize the minimal value of your act anyway.

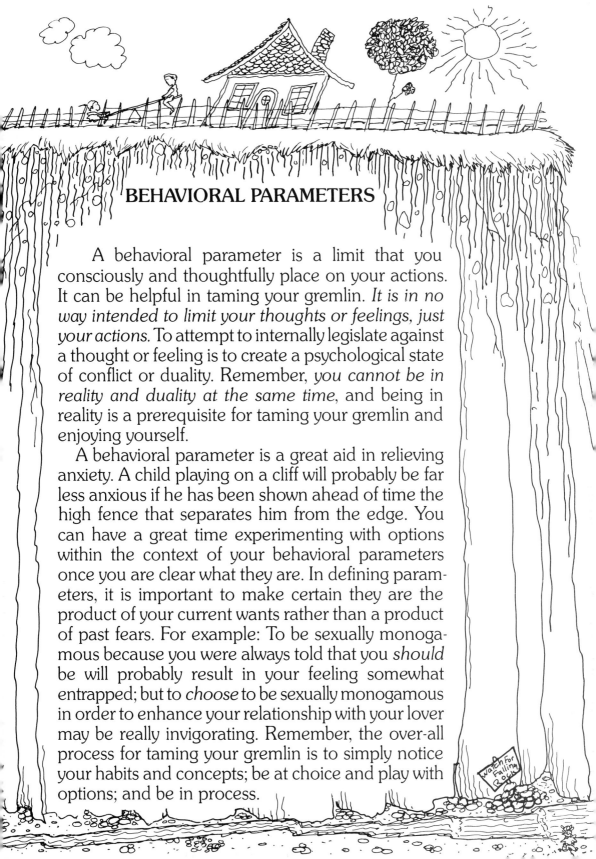

BEHAVIORAL PARAMETERS

A behavioral parameter is a limit that you consciously and thoughtfully place on your actions. It can be helpful in taming your gremlin. *It is in no way intended to limit your thoughts or feelings, just your actions.* To attempt to internally legislate against a thought or feeling is to create a psychological state of conflict or duality. Remember, *you cannot be in reality and duality at the same time*, and being in reality is a prerequisite for taming your gremlin and enjoying yourself.

A behavioral parameter is a great aid in relieving anxiety. A child playing on a cliff will probably be far less anxious if he has been shown ahead of time the high fence that separates him from the edge. You can have a great time experimenting with options within the context of your behavioral parameters once you are clear what they are. In defining parameters, it is important to make certain they are the product of your current wants rather than a product of past fears. For example: To be sexually monogamous because you *were* always told that you *should* be will probably result in your feeling somewhat entrapped; but to *choose* to be sexually monogamous in order to enhance your relationship with your lover may be really invigorating. Remember, the over-all process for taming your gremlin is to simply notice your habits and concepts; be at choice and play with options; and be in process.

GREMLIN STRATEGIES

Once you have used your awareness to ground yourself you will have a vantage point from which to detect your gremlin. Detecting and foiling your gremlin on the spot is sometimes very challenging but it is always possible. A little bit of knowledge about common gremlin strategies can enhance your awareness. Remember, to simply notice him is the first step in taming him.

The "You Can't" Strategy

This strategy, while crude and unsophisticated, has been a part of the activity of every gremlin I have encountered. In the "you can't" strategy your gremlin simply convinces you that you are not capable of attaining certain results by your actions. He knows that if you believe you have limits you will never actualize your potential. If you are unaware of your gremlin he, of course, has an obvious edge. After all, he has bombarded you with "can'ts" since before you were old enough to reason. You probably accepted them carte blanche without consideration. You may not even be aware of the "can'ts" you have accepted. Until now you may have been (and forgive me for abusing an old cliche) "too close to the forest to see the trees." As you begin to become aware of the "you can'ts" you live your life by, you may find that some are accurate: you can't fly; you can't grow taller on the spot; and you can't walk on water. Others, however, may be subtle and yet very powerful:

...beginner's luck! No way you could build another one

JONAH
and
ANDY

you can't change; you can't tame your gremlin; you can't build anything with your hands; you can't be a good athlete; you can't survive alone; you can't make money; you can't have a lasting relationship; you can't be an academic success; you can't relax; and you can't stand it (and the "it" can take infinite forms). When you hear the "you can't" or the phrase "I can't" rumbling around in your head be alert to the possible presence of your gremlin. Breathe and ground yourself. Consider rephrasing the words you have just spoken or thought, replacing the "can't" with "won't" or "will" or "choose to" or "choose not to." This will remind you of your responsibility for the limitation and in some cases of your ability to remove the limitation. When you have done this you might consider adding the words "until now" at the end or beginning of the thought or spoken phrase. The phrase "until now" is one of the most powerful tools you have for taming your gremlin. For example you might change:

I can't tell him what I feel.
    to
I choose not to tell him what I feel.
    to
Until now I have chosen not to tell him what I feel.
    to
Now I choose to tell him what I feel.

If your choice is to do as you have always done "until now" that is neither good nor bad. All that is important in this aspect of gremlin-taming is that you take responsibility for your choice. Ask yourself if your choice is based on a feared consequence or past experience rather than on the present. If so, you might wish to come out of the world of make-believe long enough to assess the validity of your fear given the current moment.

Enjoying yourself requires awareness of your freedom of choice, and the words "until now" will put you at the all-important point of *choice*. When you are not in touch with your choice in any given situation you will tend to feel trapped. Feeling trapped and enjoying yourself are hardly compatible states of being. I hope that you opt for enjoying yourself.

The "You Should,"
"You Ought-To,"
"You Must" Strategy

We have already discussed this strategy briefly, but let us review it. "Should," "must," and "ought" are gremlin terms. You may use them, too, on occasion, but your gremlin uses them frequently with the intention of trapping you in a sort of toxic duality. If you lead your life in total accordance with shoulds, ought-to's, and musts, it is as if you are a computer programmed with rules which predetermine your responses to feelings and situations. This can lead you to miss entirely the freshness, excitement, and potential for creativity inherent in living. Your gremlin will use shoulds, ought-to's, and musts to trap you in two ways:

1) Relying on fixed responses can actually make you very anxious (sometimes panicky) when you encounter intense and powerful emotions and/or situations for which your shoulds, musts, and ought-to's do not seem to apply.
2) Doing battle with the shoulds, ought-to's and musts will lock you into an internal battle with your gremlin.

Remember:

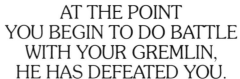

AT THE POINT
YOU BEGIN TO DO BATTLE
WITH YOUR GREMLIN,
HE HAS DEFEATED YOU.

Precisely what he wants is your attention. As long as you are interacting with him, beyond simply noticing him, your energy will not flow freely. It will be tied up in a duality. Your life will be much less enjoyable than it could be and you will be less comfortable with yourself. When you hear a "should," "must," or "ought-to" in your head consider replacing it in your thoughts and language with "choose to" or "choose not to." Again, the idea here is to channel your awareness to you

and away from your gremlin. That is, to place you "at choice." Being "at choice" will be accompanied by a feeling of excitement (perhaps hidden initially by a thin veil of fear) and an increased sense of freedom. You will still have an opportunity to make a choice but will feel less burdened, trapped, and/or anxious.

Trusting your true self instead of listening to your gremlin may feel a bit scary at first. That's natural. But so what? Change for a change. Risk trusting your true self once in a while for fun. For goodness sake, please don't let your gremlin tell you that you should or must change. Tricky devil that he is, he'll hit you with just such a paradox.

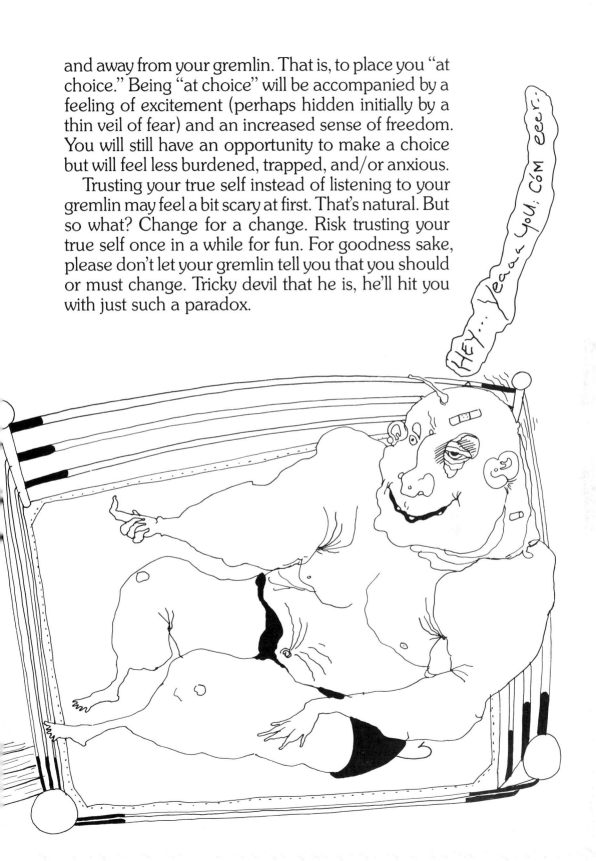

The "You Need" Strategy

When you hear yourself speaking or thinking the word "need," pay attention. It is true that you need food and water, air, shelter, and a few strokes, but most of what you imagine you need, you simply want. (Though in some cases, you may want something very badly.) Someone, sometime, started the rumor that to tell loved ones that we need them is a compliment. But, think for a moment. Would you feel better inside if someone said to you that they really "need" you, or if they said, "I really love you, and I want to be with you." Replacing the word "need" with the word "want" can be a powerful tool in taming your gremlin.

I counsel many couples who believe on a deep emotional level that they need each other. Where there is this sort of intense "need" between people there is also intense mutual resentment. It is quite beautiful and freeing when these couples begin to recognize the feeling of freedom inherent in choosing to be together rather than needing to be together.

Something about this slight shift in the flavor of a relationship allows people the space to really begin loving one another. An image I have had on several occasions, while working with couples who were feeling very "needy," is reminiscent of two pets I once had. When my cats, Sophie and Jesse, were kittens they used to play actively on the floor. Sophie and Jesse looked to me as if they were wrestling. They would place their forepaws on each other's neck as they rolled over and over on the floor. In a way, it appeared that they were hugging one another, the whole while licking and chewing on each other's face. They looked really happy. What I noticed also, however, was that while they were "making nice" and playing with the upper parts of their bodies, they were, with their back paws, clawing the devil out of one another's stomach. Somehow this image seems appropriate when I encounter couples who think they need each other. Replacing the word "need" with the word "want" can be helpful in taming your gremlin.

The "You Don't Deserve" Strategy

In this strategy your gremlin will simply convince you that you are not worthy of something you want, be it a material thing, a good time, or perpetual enjoyment. He will do all in his power to make you feel undeserving, afraid, or guilty. Simply remember, guilt serves not one positive purpose. Think of your guilt as an IOU. Either tear it up or ask yourself whom it is you owe and what it is you owe them. Make a reasonable decision as to what act, if any, you want to perform in order to allow yourself to tear it up and then perform the act as quickly as possible. Tear up the IOU. This will send your gremlin scurrying and alleviate guilt. Keep in mind, you deserve whatever you want and you may want whatever you choose to want. With your freedom of choice comes responsibility, so remember, you are responsible for your choices.

HAPPY day I

The "Fantasy Is Reality" Strategy

Your gremlin loves the idea of having you lead your life based on assumptions. The world of make-believe is his turf. Sometimes simply taking the time to accurately phrase your processes as you notice them will send your gremlin running and bring you from fantasy into reality and hence to the all-important point of choice. If, for example, you feel that your boss will reject an idea that you really want to share with him, you might say to yourself, "I am imagining that my boss will reject my idea." It is important that you emphasize the word *imagine*, for what you are after is a heightened awareness of the process whereby your gremlin is frightening you. You can explore your fantasy to whatever depth you choose by following this thought process format and filling in the blanks accordingly.

If I _____,
    #1 (action you are afraid to take)

I IMAGINE that _____.
        #2 (consequence)

If _____,
    Insert response from #2

I IMAGINE that _____.
        #3 (consequence)

If _____,
    Insert response from #3

I IMAGINE that _____.
        #4 (consequence)

You can carry this exercise as far as you like. Often you will see an element of absurdity in your fears and will notice that on a deep emotional level you are basing your action or lack of it on a fear of abandonment, or of death. As you look closely at the situation you may be able to see that the potential for these

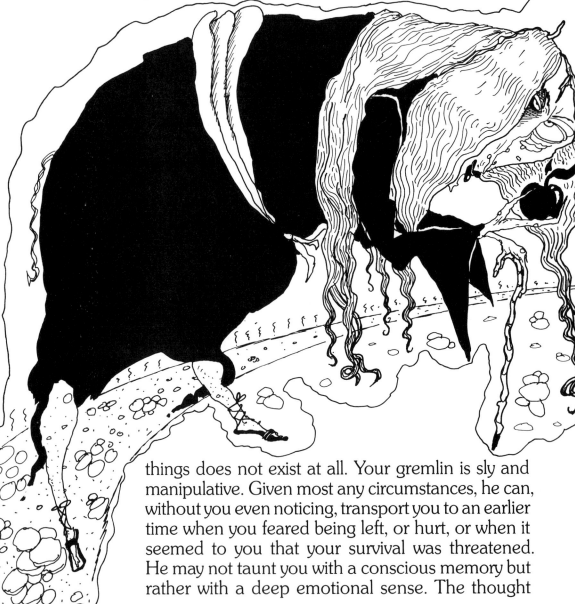

things does not exist at all. Your gremlin is sly and manipulative. Given most any circumstances, he can, without you even noticing, transport you to an earlier time when you feared being left, or hurt, or when it seemed to you that your survival was threatened. He may not taunt you with a conscious memory but rather with a deep emotional sense. The thought process format I have suggested will accent the process whereby your gremlin is scaring you and will help you to escape from the world of make-believe. This will afford you some clarity and perspective from which to choose your action.

Accenting the process whereby your gremlin is

scaring you will diminish the fear. I am not sure why or how this works but I believe it is related to the existential theory of change we discussed earlier:

"I change not by trying to be
something other than I am;
I change by becoming
fully aware of how I am."

It may be simply that, like the proverbial child with his hand caught in the cookie jar, your gremlin, once caught, becomes embarrassed and stops what he is doing. Once your fear is diminished you may still choose not to take a risk. This is ginger-peachy, but at least your choice is based on realistic considerations such as timing and real consequences rather than on a habit formed long ago, or on unrealistic fantasies about the future. The old adage "anxiety is the gap between the now and the then" applies here.

One much overlooked option for determining whether or not to risk making a statement to someone, is to check out your considerations by stating them aloud. You might, for example, say to your boss, "I have an idea I'd like to share with you, and I'm not sure how open you would be to my suggestion. Would you like to hear my suggestion?"; or, "I have an idea I'm considering sharing with you. When and how would be the best way to do that?"; or, "I have an idea I'd like to share with you and get your thoughts on. It needs some refinement. I think it might benefit the company in the long run if you will apply your expertise to it." These sorts of statements are not panaceas—just options. And even thinking them out to yourself without verbalizing them often can be very freeing. Now, don't let your gremlin tell you that you should or must change, or that you should or must take risks. Instead: simply notice; choose and play with options; and be in process.

The "They Have to Change in Order for Me to Feel Better" Strategy

The "They Have to Change in Order for Me to Feel Better" strategy is, for most gremlins, an age-old favorite. The "they" referred to in this strategy can mean people or circumstances. In operationalizing this strategy your gremlin wants you to waste energy in one of two ways, either by worrying or by knocking yourself out to change people and circumstances. It is important to be able to determine when such an activity can be productive and when it is an out-and-out waste of time, remembering that your primary goal is to feel good and *enjoy yourself*. NOTHING is more beneficial to a clear sense of self-enjoyment than an awareness of where you end and the rest of the world begins. There are always going to be disturbances to you as an organism and some of these disturbances will engender in you a great deal of discomfort; but wouldn't it be nice if you could learn to enjoy yourself in the midst of all sorts of seemingly abrasive circumstances? You can, by learning to ground yourself as I have suggested and by practicing separating out what you actually see and hear going on around you from the implications and fantasies your gremlin gleans from these circumstances. Remember, your gremlin prefers that you focus your awareness on fantasies and assumptions.

Once, several years ago, I was being Rolfed. Rolfing involves very deep massage and can be a painful and intense physical experience. It is a process in which a trained practitioner physically softens and smoothes out the connective tissue formed around the body's muscles. During the Rolfing session, I noticed myself tensing as the Rolfer was working very deeply on my abdominal muscles. I feared being hurt. By the same token, I knew that the deeper I could allow the Rolfer to work, the more I would benefit from the session. I began to notice my tendency to tense my body at the anticipation of pain—rather than in response to the pain itself. I was tensing in an effort to somehow defend myself against pain. This sort of tense attempt at preparedness is almost valueless. On the other hand, when we are in a state of relaxed concentration our bodies are more likely to move in fine accordance to the demands made upon them. As I relaxed more the Rolfer was able to work deeper and deeper. When I actually felt pain my body tensed very naturally—but not until the pain actually occurred. My pain and tension were diminished by the end of the session. I enjoyed myself, and I benefited more than I might have. Your gremlin wants you to believe that tensing against emotional pain before it occurs will minimize the discomfort. Actually, this extends it. In interpersonal relationships this sort of defensiveness tends to create and exacerbate unpleasantness.

As you begin to truly recognize the benefits of enjoying yourself, you will want to enjoy yourself as much of the time as possible. At the point your level of self-enjoyment is the least bit dampened, you will want to revive it as quickly as you can. This does not mean that it will benefit you once you have noticed you are not enjoying yourself to begin *acting* as if you are enjoying yourself. A plastic grin or the proverbial stiff upper lip has no place in true enjoyment. Rather, the challenge is to return to a place of true self-comfort and enjoyment as quickly as possible without blocking or avoiding your feelings. If you block or avoid your feelings you will feel unfinished and tense. Remember, blocking your feelings is not the same as resolving them, and unresolved feelings will re-emerge and negatively affect your level of enjoyment. Instead of blocking your feelings: simply notice them; make a conscious choice as to what to do with them (without overlooking the option of simply feeling them); and play with options.

There is value sometimes in modifying circum-stances that appear to be disturbing your sense of enjoyment. Often, however, it is easier to regulate your own moods and reactions. It takes less time. When something in your environment affects you directly, be it a hug, a kiss, criticism, bad weather, a car wreck, a loud noise or whatever, you will feel it in your body. The effects may be short lived or long lasting. If the effect is a negative one, that is, one that doesn't feel good to you and diverts you from enjoying yourself, your gremlin will do all in his power to make it last as long as possible. He will even encourage you to focus your awareness on unpleasant circumstances that need have no effect on you at all. Your gremlin will make mountains out of mole hills and encourage you to spend time in your head considering the ins and outs of external situations toward the futile goal of making yourself right, making yourself wrong, planning revenge or justifying an action. Basically, what he wants is for you to waste time in the interest of preserving a concept (about you or about the world), or a habit (for responding to feelings or to people). *He will convince you that preserving your concepts and habits is the same as preserving your life.*

When your gremlin has you occupied with these activities, you will observe (if you are aware) that you are not enjoying yourself. At these points in time you have a choice. You can do nothing, modify your circumstances, or modify your mood.

IT IS MORE IMPORTANT THAT YOU BE ABLE TO REGULATE ENJOYMENT WITHIN YOURSELF REGARDLESS OF CIRCUMSTANCES, THAN IT IS FOR YOU TO BE ABLE TO MODIFY CIRCUMSTANCES; IT SIMPLY COMES IN HANDY MORE OFTEN.

It takes practice to develop the ability to do this expediently and smoothly, but it is a very valuable skill to have.

When you are grounded (as we discussed earlier) you are able to experience yourself as a vibrating alive essence encased within a body. Your experience when you are in this state may be as if you are peering out from your body into a three-dimensional world which surrounds you, and of which you are a part. You will have a sense of detachment. This in no way implies a sense of not-caring or of isolation. On the contrary, when you allow yourself to experience where you end and the rest of the world begins, you are able to see the rest of the world much more clearly. In terms of interpersonal relationships, you will find that you are able to love much more unconditionally, and to be more accepting. This sense will allow you to see that your gremlin is responsible for much of your misery. This sense will also enable you to lessen the degree of blaming you do of those around you. Those around you may be obnoxious, mean, stubborn, whiny, and inconsiderate from time to time, but in many instances the misery you feel as a result of their behavior is something you can learn to remove within a few seconds. Reminding yourself that you aren't perfect either is helpful. (How's that for heavy-duty psychology?) But what helps even more is grounding yourself. Practice grounding yourself in tense circumstances. It can be enjoyable. Remember that grounding yourself is something that you can learn to do very easily and quickly with practice. To ground yourself you must have the desire and the intention to ground yourself. When interpersonal conflict is involved, this may require that you let go of a desire to *be right.*

When you become aware that your gremlin has convinced you that being right is important, ask yourself what you have to gain from being right. Usually the intensity with which you want to be right is matched by the intensity with which you are clinging to a concept of who you are and more specifically, a concept of who you are in your relationship to the person or persons with whom you are in conflict. Be absolutely, even frightfully, honest with yourself. You will probably gain some clarity as to what concept you are momentarily devoting your life to preserving.

Having simply noticed that you are invested in being right, become aware of how it feels in your body; then make a choice. Your options are infinite, but again the most obvious ones are: to fight like hell to prove your point; to let the other person be right; to drop your desire to be right; or to play with an option that sounds like fun, remembering that all you really want to do is enjoy yourself in process anyway.

The "Hem and Haw" Strategy

When you are "busting" to say something but are afraid of the consequences of doing so, your gremlin may encourage you to *hem and haw*. I have had clients whose gremlins have scared them into developing highly sophisticated hem and haw techniques. One of my clients utilized an amazing sense of timing, an authoritative voice, a wide vocabulary, and the phrases "Know what I mean?" and "You know?" to get one or more listeners to nod their heads in agreement to his tirades of verbal nonsense. This method of "non-communication" comprised, in part, his act of Benevolent Philosopher. He had many acquaintances but felt that no one really knew him. Had he been at all grounded and in touch with himself, he would have physically detected his gremlin, for hem-and-hawers often develop a feeling of tightness in their stomachs, an aching head, shortness of breath, and a general feeling of discontent. Also, had he been willing to quit hemming and hawing long enough to notice, he might have seen puzzled looks, people leaving the room, and plastic, ineffectual smiles. But that's the way it is with gremlins. They sneak up

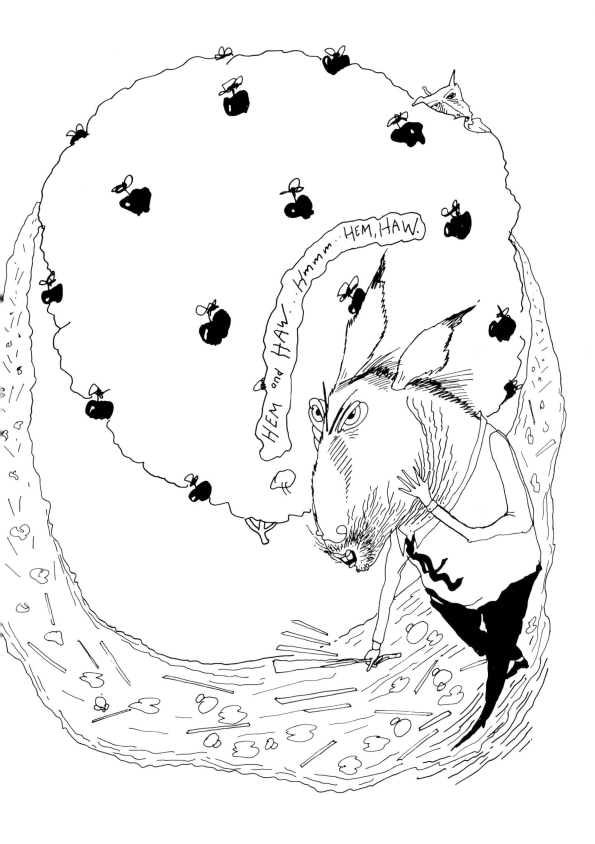

on us when we least expect them and suddenly and secretly trap us into behaviors which, when objectively witnessed, are downright embarrassing. We, of course, don't know what we don't know. When we are hemming and hawing our gremlin has convinced us to let slide our all-important tools of simply noticing; choosing and playing with options; and being in process. Fortunately for us, at the point we see our gremlin in action we can tame him on the spot. To foil the hem and haw strategy we need only to become aware of our wants, our thoughts, and our feelings, and to state them clearly and concisely. Like most methods for foiling your gremlin on the spot, this is a very simple one; so simple that it is often overlooked. A simple sentence is far more profound than an elaborate analogy or explanation when it comes to making yourself understood and to putting your gremlin in his place. If what is true in a particular instance is that you want to hide yourself rather than express yourself, that is fine. Simply make the choice to do so instead of hemming and hawing. When you hem and haw, or "peek and hide" as some of my clients have called it, you risk looking like a babbling idiot. That's probably not what you want, but it is probably what your gremlin wants. Remember, when you are feeling one thing and expressing another, you are being phony and when you are being phony, your phoniness is probably obvious to those around you.

If you want to say something but you are feeling afraid or cautious, mentally acknowledge the consequence you fear and consider stating it (the consequence) aloud. Often this level of intense honesty will shock your gremlin into a state of temporary immobilization. With your gremlin immobilized, the *fear* of unpredictability will become the *excitement* of unpredictability. You will be in touch with your freedom to say precisely what you mean. Knowing what it is you want to say and saying it clearly and concisely is usually a good idea. Hemming and hawing is good for no one and will seldom get you what you want.

When you communicate clearly, instead of hemming and hawing, you will feel much more alive and you will open to yourself the possibility of intimacy and warmth in your relationships. When you hem and haw you avoid the potential for the growth and unpredictability that is inherent in every human relationship. Your relationships will become predictable, superficial, and boring. A relationship is a system and as in any system, when there are no new inputs, the system enters a state of entropy or degradation. Risk-taking and new inputs into human relationships are essential if the relationship is going to thrive and deepen. Following are some rules your gremlin would love to have you follow, as he knows they will insure for you shallow relationships and perpetual disappointment:

1. Use generalizations such as "we" and the terms "you," or "people" instead of the term "I."
2. Confuse feeling with thinking.
3. Conceptualize problematic situations in such a way as to make others responsible for your misery.

4. Smile when you are angry and sad.
5. Use "can't" when you mean "won't."
6. Lead your life in accordance with rules and regulations and without taking into account your natural desires and the current moment.
7. Make an effort to keep relationships comfortable and predictable; and, for goodness sake, don't rock the boat.
8. Relate to those close to you as you have always related to them.
9. Assume that you know what others are thinking and feeling.
10. Never disagree.
11. Be clear about the roles others expect you to play, and make certain not to engender in them any discomfort by doing something unpredictable.
12. Confuse wants and needs.

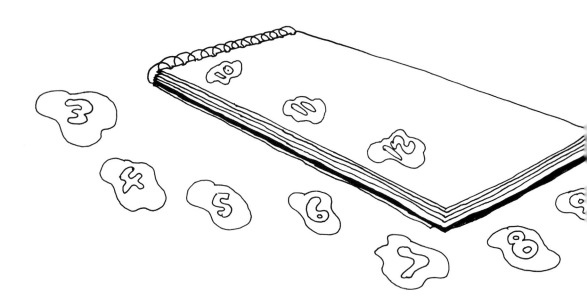

The
"My Fear Is
Scaring Me to Death"
Strategy

In this strategy your gremlin will convince you that you are about to die. This is a cruel and vicious strategy used by gremlins when they are feeling desperate. I once had a client named Hank who had a family history of heart disease. He had been warned by the media that he was a Type A personality. His anxiety over having a heart attack was tremendous; yet, he knew that the last thing he needed was anxiety. He became anxious about his anxiety. The whole cycle perpetuated itself until Hank began to have one anxiety attack after another. These usually took the form of chest pains. On several occasions he rushed himself to the emergency room. He had electrocardiograms and general medical workups done, all of which determined that there was nothing medically wrong with his heart. In our work together, Hank developed a mechanism for taming his gremlin on the spot. He simply grounded himself and began to listen to his gremlin. He allowed his gremlin from 5 to 10 minutes of monologue. He listened to all that his gremlin had to say. On occasion, he verbalized all of his gremlin's statements. Once, in my office, he allowed his gremlin to talk and the dialogue sounded something like this: "Well, now you've done it. Boy, your family's sure going to miss you. You're going to croak any minute. Look at you, you're a nervous wreck. You're too fat. You smoke too much. Your breathing is shallow. You're scared to death—really scared. You're a total sissy. Actually, you're a whiny baby. I can't for the life of me imagine how you've lived this long. You don't deserve to be where you are. The only reason you even have a job is because your boss can't see through you. If people in this world really knew you they'd see that you're just a fat slob. You can't keep up this pressure forever, Buddy. You're probably going to lose your job tomorrow and your wife's getting a little fed up with you anyway. She may leave you. She's probably having an affair right now. And your kids don't like you. You're losing total control over them." And on and on and on.

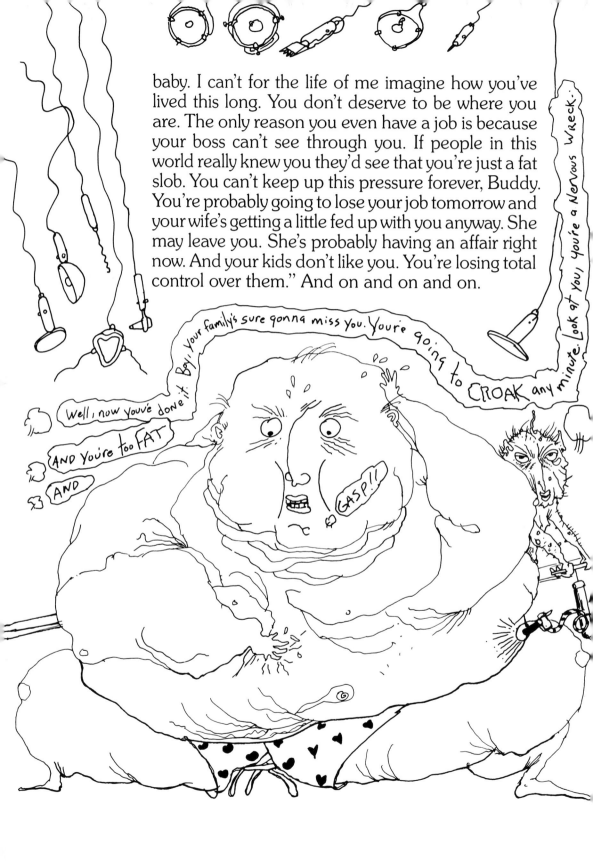

Boy! your family's sure gonna miss you. You're going to CROAK any minute. Look at you, you're a Nervous Wreck.

Well, now you've done it.

AND You're too FAT

AND

GASP!!

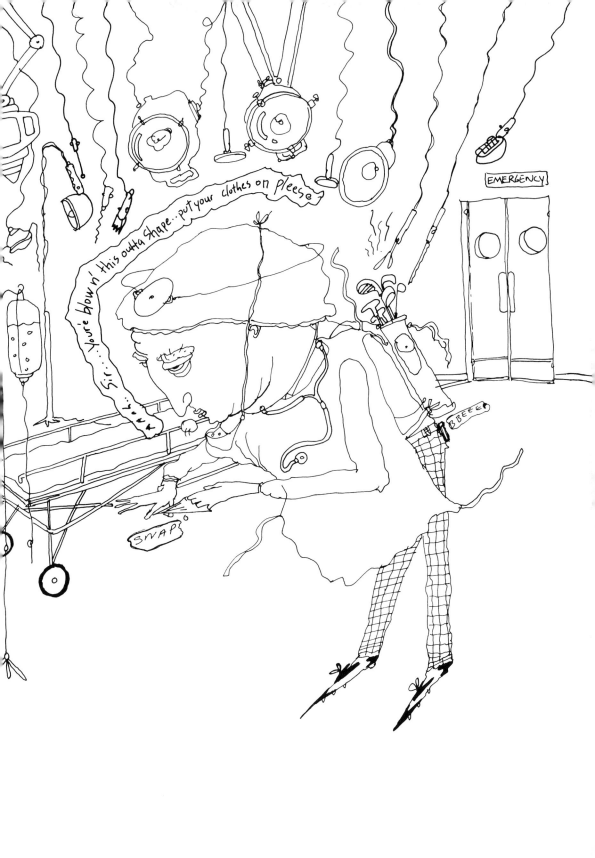

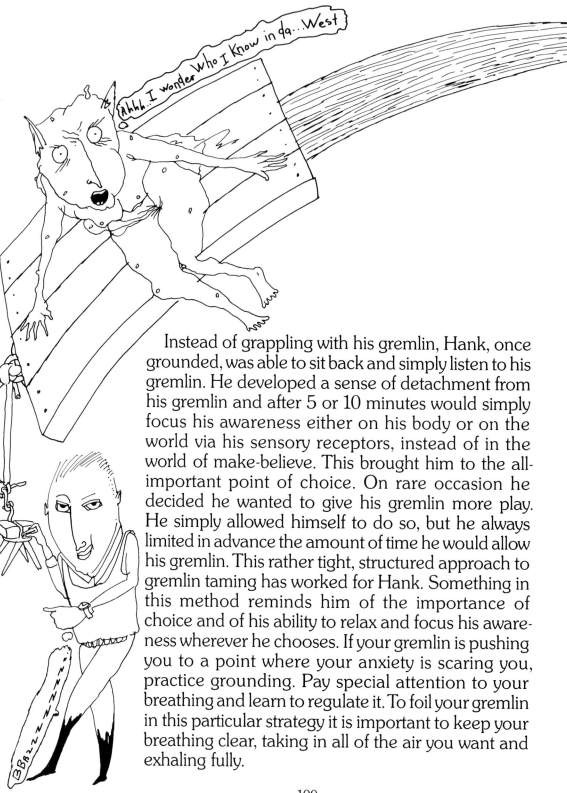

Ahhh...I wonder who I know in da...West

BBRzzzzzzz

Instead of grappling with his gremlin, Hank, once grounded, was able to sit back and simply listen to his gremlin. He developed a sense of detachment from his gremlin and after 5 or 10 minutes would simply focus his awareness either on his body or on the world via his sensory receptors, instead of in the world of make-believe. This brought him to the all-important point of choice. On rare occasion he decided he wanted to give his gremlin more play. He simply allowed himself to do so, but he always limited in advance the amount of time he would allow his gremlin. This rather tight, structured approach to gremlin taming has worked for Hank. Something in this method reminds him of the importance of choice and of his ability to relax and focus his aware-ness wherever he chooses. If your gremlin is pushing you to a point where your anxiety is scaring you, practice grounding. Pay special attention to your breathing and learn to regulate it. To foil your gremlin in this particular strategy it is important to keep your breathing clear, taking in all of the air you want and exhaling fully.

Thus far we have discussed the value of simply noticing our habits and concepts, and of playing with options. Remember the "simply" in "simply noticing" and the "playing" in "playing with options" as you learn more about the gremlin taming process and enjoying yourself. Before reading on you might wish to reflect for a moment on what you have learned about:

Being Grounded;
Guiding Your Awareness;
Habits and Concepts;
Being at Choice;
Selecting Options for Expression;
Behavioral Parameters; and
Gremlin Strategies—remembering that gremlin taming is an on-going adventure.

5

BEING IN PROCESS

Making a conscious decision to see taming your gremlin as an on-going adventure that will be forever "in process" is an essential part of enjoying yourself. There is no finish line when it comes to gremlin taming. Yet, your gremlin wants you to believe

that your happiness lies somewhere in the future as a reward to be granted once you have arranged your actions and the people and circumstances of your life into just the right configuration. As you, however, begin to tame your gremlin you will gain an appreciation for the simple truth that happiness is not a static state—an entity to be captured. Rather, it is an experience that, like emptiness, is always available and accessible. Being *in process* is an attitude—an appreciation of this simple truth and of the reality that your life will be forever unfolding and your future always unknown. Allowing yourself to acknowledge that this is what is so may be unsettling, but as you tame your gremlin this fact of life will become not only palatable but invigorating. Seeing yourself as *in process* will aid you in increasing your level of self-enjoyment.

Simply noticing; choosing and playing with options; and being in process are states of being that are available to you from moment to moment. You will never tame your gremlin forever, be miserable forever, or insure your happiness forever. At every moment you have a choice: to heed the words of your gremlin or to be in harmony with your true essence. The option to enjoy yourself will never dry up and blow away. It is an option that is available to you in every instant, as is the choice to let your gremlin interfere with your self-enjoyment. So long as you are willing to ground yourself and to *simply notice*, you will never lose the vantage point of the current moment, and from this home base of operation you can always choose to tame your gremlin. Every moment holds in it the potential for complete self-enjoyment and for complete misery. The choice is yours. Taming your gremlin and enjoying yourself is an on-going, moment-to-moment process.

6

FOR KICKS

As I've mentioned, gremlins change their styles, appearances, methods, and even their sex from time to time. With that recognition and just for kicks, you might want to do a rough sketch of your gremlin as you imagine him or her at this point in time. What does he look like? Has he a color? Is he large or small; slim or heavy; mean looking; vague; distinct? On one of the blank pages in the back of the book, you might want to create a visual representation of your gremlin. Does he remind you of the Coach, the Artist, the Reverend, or any of the other gremlins I shared with you earlier? He may even remind you of someone you know. Give him a name if you wish. Remember that gremlins change their style and form rather often. A sketch from time to time might be a good idea. If you are unable to visualize your gremlin — that is fine. Don't fret. Relax.

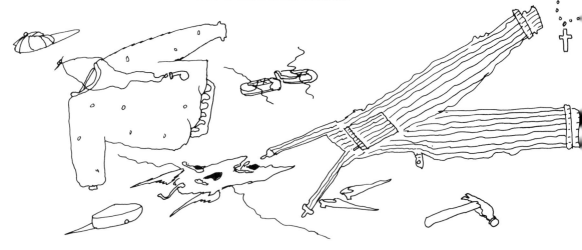

Another excellent method for getting a handle on your gremlin is to write an introduction of him. In fact, you might actually introduce him, via a detailed description, to a friend and then assist your friend in identifying his or her gremlin.

Your relationship with your gremlin will be a lifelong one. Start now to acknowledge him fully, remembering that acknowledgment and entanglement are not the same. Simply notice him and the habits for responding to feelings and people that he insists you lead your life by. Notice the concepts on which these habits are based and notice, too, the effect of your gremlin's presence on your body, your relationships, and of course on your overall level of enjoyment. Choose and play with options for expression once in a while. Change for a change, and enjoy being in the process of gremlin taming.

7

THE PLEASANT PERSON ACT

Acting can be fun so long as you are clear that you are not your act. A good act can get you some strokes, can help you get elected to office, can help you win friends, and can even help you make money. Some of the most uptight people I know have good acts, so please, if you should get into acting, don't take yourself too seriously. You risk a feeling of real emptiness. Acting should be thought of as either experimentation, conscious pretentiousness, a good time, or an out-and-out manipulation.

Some acts are, of course, better than others. One of the most popular is the Pleasant Person Act. I asked several of my clients and colleagues about this act. All were aware of it and some have used it as a base from which they have created their own unique performing style. I was surprised by the degree of agreement I found among those I consulted as to the essential attributes of the Pleasant Person Act. Here they are:

Listen more than you talk;
Speak softly but audibly;
Don't repeat yourself;
Use no more words than are necessary;
Make eye-contact without staring;
Pay attention to what you see;
Don't chew your moustache (or anyone else's);

106

Brush your teeth at least twice a day;
Don't eat onions or garlic before social
  engagements;
Smell good;
Don't make noises when you breathe;
Breathe fully but not heavily;
Sit straight, but not rigid;
Dress in clothes that fit you and feel good;
Don't brag;
Be friendly;
Shake hands firmly but don't overdo it;
Verbally acknowledge your discomfort
  when you notice it;
Verbally acknowledge your lack of under-
  standing when you feel it;
Ask questions and marvel at the answers;
Be kind to animals;
Don't repeat yourself;
Look for things to like and comment on
  them;
Keep your body and hair clean;
Make a daily check list of things to do;
Don't do two of them;
Do the rest;
Exercise every day;
When having a conversation with a child,
  kneel down to his or her eye level;
Don't expect children to act like adults;
Don't call people names;
Don't talk bad behind people's back;
To a third party say something nice about
  someone else;
Keep your body relaxed;
Don't force a smile;
Don't interrupt;
Go slow;

Don't repeat yourself;
Don't be a monotone;
Use good grammar;
Be respectful to ALL old folks,
        no exceptions;

When people visit you, make them
        comfortable;
Do not wear too much cologne or perfume;
Keep agreements;
Respect others' beliefs;
Do more than your part to keep the planet
        clean;
Keep the temperature nice in your dwelling;
Wake up early;
Don't pick your teeth (or your nose) in
        public;

Don't clean your nails in public;
Cover your mouth when you cough;
Cover your mouth and your nose with a
        handkerchief when you sneeze;
Leave well enough alone;
Remember names;

Don't tell ethnic jokes or make racial slurs;
Ask clearly and explicitly for what you want;
Take responsibility for being clearly
        understood;
Listen carefully to what others say;
Ask for clarification when you are uncertain;
Write legibly;
Don't ask rhetorical questions;
Don't overeat;

Be in the midst of learning something
        new;
Accept what is obvious;
Change your routine once a week (change
        this routine once in a while);

Avoid sugar without being obsessive
about it;
Give up trying to be something special;
Don't smoke;
Don't get stumbly drunk or slur your words;
Don't physically hurt any living thing;
When in a dialogue, get in touch with that
part of you that is nosey but not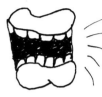
intrusive, remembering that real life
is far more interesting than television;
Don't be anxious to verbalize a parallel
from your own experience;
Don't act out your joy to the point of being
phony; and
Don't let your sadness turn you into the
kind of grump who is a pain in the
ass to be with;
Do not use hair slickum;
Don't repeat yourself.

    How about adding to this list a few of your own
notions relevant to The Pleasant Person Act? You
might want to use this information as a basis for
shoring up your own act, so make sure that what you
write comes from you and not from your gremlin.
Use the blank pages at the back of this book if you
wish. Remember, you are not your act.

8

A FINAL WORD

More and more I am having the experience of separateness from my gremlin and, as a result, I am fully enjoying more of each day. The payoff for me in writing this book is in my enjoyment of the process. The process has included some vague fantasies of future recognition, money, love, and security, so I know that my gremlin is doing his best to set me up for falling into his grasp. He is so persistent. Yet, I don't fear him. Something very beautiful is happening in my life when I experience the real me instead of my gremlin. With that as my focus, I feel incredibly happy. My intellectual notion (half-baked idea, wild-eyed fantasy from the world of make-believe) is that I will one day be entirely one with my essence and free from my gremlin.

Even now I sometimes "do action" with the feeling that I am flowing in complete harmony with my true self. It is the best feeling I know. I feel it at this moment. Often I have this experience when I am writing or talking about my essence. Becoming more and more in tune with my essence is the main event of my life. I see clearly that it can be done (actually, allowed to *do me* is probably much more accurate), not once and for all, but time after time, day after day, moment after moment. We can all have the ultimately beautiful experience of this existence—not a catharsis or satori, not an insight, not a hallucinogenic flash, not a Zen moment, not even a religious revelation, but a pure and constant, readily available experience of our purest essence.

As I have mentioned I am more a student than a teacher of this process—a preschooler at best. <u>Taming Your Gremlin: a Guide to Enjoying Yourself</u> has been my way of sharing my experience and my perceptions. Should you choose to get about the business of enjoying yourself and of taming your gremlin, I would like to hear from you. Simply noticing; choosing and playing with options; and being in process have, for me, been powerful tools in the art of gremlin taming. I hope that they will be for you. I wish you relaxed concentration and happiness. Share your experience with others and above all, enjoy yourself.

About the Author

Richard Carson lives near Dallas with his wife, Leti, and their son, Jonah. He writes out of his thirteen years as a psychotherapist and as a consultant to human service professionals. His professional background includes service as a full-time faculty member for the University of Texas Southwestern Medical School, and as an Adjunct Assistant Professor for the University of Texas at Arlington Graduate School of Social Work. He is a Clinical Member and Approved Supervisor of the American Association for Marriage and Family Therapy, a Licensed Professional Counselor in Texas, and a Certified Social Worker with an Order of Recognition as an Advanced Clinical Practitioner. Richard is a member of the Academy of Certified Social Workers. He consults and conducts seminars across the nation for a myriad of institutions, agencies, organizations and businesses, and may be reached at 7424 Greenville Avenue, Suite 113, Dallas, TX 75231 (214) 363-0788.

NOTES